FENG SHUI

A COMPLETE GUIDE

Richard Craze

Acknowledgements

The author would like to thank Roni Jay for her invaluable editorial assistance, love, kindness and tolerance, in preparing this book; the Hong Kong Tourist Association for its kind permission to reproduce the photograph of the lo p'an; and Chu Lin for his guidance and teaching on all aspects of feng shui.

About the author

Richard Craze is a freelance writer specialising in books on Chinese culture, religion and complementary health. Some of his other books include:

Feng Shui for beginners (Hodder & Stoughton, 1995)
The Feng Shui Pack (HarperCollins, Godsfield Press, 1997)
Practical Feng Shui (Anness Publishing Ltd, 1997)
The Feng Shui Game Pack (HarperCollins, Godsfield Press, 1997)
Teach Yourself Traditional Chinese Medicine (Hodder & Stoughton, 1997)
Chinese Herbal Medicine (Piatkus, 1995)
Herbal Teas (Quintet, 1997)
The Spiritual Traditions of Sex (Godsfield Press, 1996)
Tantric Sexuality – a beginner's guide (Hodder & Stoughton, 1997)
Teach Yourself Chinese Astrology (Hodder & Stoughton, 1997)
Teach Yourself Alexander Technique (Hodder & Stoughton, 1996)

Order queries: please contact Bookpoint Ltd, 39 Milton Park, Abingdon, Oxon OX14 4TD. Telephone: (44) 01235 400414, Fax: (44) 01235 400454. Lines are open from 9.00 – 6.00, Monday to Saturday, with a 24 hour message answering service. Email address: orders@bookpoint.co.uk

British Library Cataloguing in Publication Data
A catalogue record for this title is available from The British Library

ISBN 0 340 69708 3

First published 1997

Impression number	13	12	11	10	9	8	7	6	5	4	3	
Year		20003	2002	2001	2000		1999		1998		1997	

Copyright © 1997 Richard Craze

Typeset by Transet Limited, Coventry, England.

Printed in Great Britain for Hodder & Stoughton Educational, a division of Hodder Headline plc, 338 Euston Road, London NW1 3BH by Cox & Wyman, Reading, Berkshire.

CONTENTS

INTRODUCTION

Hoc erat in votis: modus agri non ita magnus,
Hortus ubi et tecto vicinus iugis aquae fons
Et paulum silvae super his foret.
*This was one of my prayers: for a parcel of land not so
very large, which should have a garden and a spring of
ever-flowing water near the house, and a bit of
woodland as well as these.*

HORACE, 65–8 BCE

Defining feng shui

What is feng shui? Put simply, feng shui is the art of learning
to live in harmony with our surroundings – being a part of
nature rather than a blot on the landscape. It may seem
strange that we humans have to learn how to do this. After
all, other animals certainly don't. You only have to think
about how at home they seem in their natural habitat to
realise how bizarre and out of place we have become.
Hardly any of us could survive for too long without all the
devices that society places at our disposal – I know I couldn't
survive one night out in the wilds without heat and light and
coffee. We need to wear clothes whereas other animals
don't; we need to be fed as small infants for a far greater
time than almost any other animal; we aren't even self-sufficient
for nearly 20 years; we have no natural habitat; and we need
constant protection from the weather and nature in general.
At times it may seem as if we don't even really belong on
this planet. But we do. And feng shui is the Chinese art of
getting the maximum benefit from our surroundings.

1

A few basic rules

We can learn, quite simply, a few basic rules that govern the best possible use of our environment to enable us to prosper and be healthy. These rules may seem, at first glance, to be strangely different from what we are used to, as they are coming from a completely different culture, but after a short while they become second nature. The rules of feng shui are based on thousands of years of observation and experimentation over countless millions of lifetimes. These are firm and proven methods of changing and improving the way we live to give us all that we need without recourse to too much expense or having to change too much. All we have to do is observe the way we live now and how we feel about our lives. If everything is fine then we need to change nothing. If, however, there is any area of our lives that needs improvement then feng shui can help us.

Luck management

For most of us there will be some area that certainly needs improving. Maybe it's our relationships that need a little assistance, or our wealth or career that could do with a helping hand. Feng shui is about taking control, placing responsibility back in our own hands. No longer can we moan about our fate or luck. Feng shui is, as the Chinese say, luck management, and once we have the means at our disposal we can manage our luck supremely well.

Once we start to learn about the principles of feng shui it will quickly become apparent that it permeates every aspect of our lives, from where we live to our workplace, from our gardens to our health. Feng shui has many strands that connect us to nature. By learning to live in harmony with nature we can use all its resources. If, however, we are out of harmony, out of balance, then we will suffer reduced luck. And luck is not a chance happening. It is the result of learning the rules of nature and living by them:

understanding how energy moves around us and using that information to improve our supply of luck. There's nothing lucky about luck – it's all a question of management.

The principles of feng shui

And the rules of feng shui aren't even rules – they're merely well tried pieces of advice. The good thing about feng shui is that you can do so much for yourself. If it works, carry on doing it – if it doesn't then you can try something else. The principles of feng shui are based on a knowledge of *ch'i, yin* and *yang*, the five elements and the eight compass directions. There's nothing difficult to learn. Some of it may at first appear strange to Westerners but the beauty of feng shui is that you don't have to believe anything. The principles are what they are – they don't require any input from us. If we believe in them then that's all well and good. If we don't believe in them then that's fine as well. The principles will carry on working without any help from us. I know of some followers of feng shui who have said that they don't know how it works, don't understand it and can't really believe that it can work – but then confess that it works for them – as it will for you. There's no magic in it and no philosophy. You try it and if you notice an improvement then it has worked. Feng shui is safe and practical. There's nothing to harm you or make things worse. You can only improve or remain static. And the second you begin to effect change you will affect change. The mere act of noticing how you live, your surroundings and environment, is almost enough to cause the changes to begin at once.

In the following chapters we will look at a brief history of feng shui, the principles of feng shui, and practical applications of feng shui. The history is there to remind you that you are dealing with a skill that has been carried out in China and allied cultures for thousands of years. There is nothing new or invented about this. It is all tried and tested. Perhaps some of the interpretations will vary as times change but the fundamental elements underlying feng shui certainly don't change. The principles are there so you will have a grounding in the philosophy of Taoism, which is the ancient religion or belief system of old China. Feng shui is the practical side of Taoism – putting into practice the beliefs of a culture that has endured almost without change for 3,000 years at least. The Taoist's beliefs are simple and make extraordinary sense even today. And again there is no need to take on anyone else's belief system. Try it and if it works carry on doing it.

Taoism and feng shui

Although Taoism may originally have been perceived as a religion by early Western visitors to China, it is more and yet less. More because it permeates every facet of life – and less because it is not a true religion; there is no God to believe in (or not believe in); there is no creed or dogma; there isn't even a hierarchy or priesthood. Taoism is just a simple and workable philosophy of how the universe is put together, how it functions and our place in it. By using the principles of Taoism (and by that very nature also the principles of feng shui) we can learn to flow more harmoniously with nature instead of being in opposition and fighting nature. Nature is about energy and the way energy flows. Feng shui is about nature and the way nature flows. The Taoists believe that the energy of life flows according to certain principles. They called the energy *ch'i*. We can learn, by practising feng shui, how ch'i flows and how to make use of its abundance.

In this book we will try to work through as many practical applications as possible, but don't worry if your exact living space is not described. There is an old Chinese saying – 'give a man a fish and you feed him for a day; teach him to fish and you feed him for life'. I am not going to give you a fish; I am going to teach you to fish: teach you how feng shui works so you can put its principles into practice no matter how or where you live and work.

Once you have learnt the principles you will find you can apply them to any area of your life; it's a question of learning to stand back and see how the energy flows around a particular area. If the flow is harmonious and correct then you can only benefit in that area. If the flow is stunted, corrupted or interrupted then it's logical that the area will also be adversely affected. Once we learn how the energy flow should be we can make sure it is correct. There are various remedies you can carry out in your home or office that can modify the flow of energy to make it more harmonious. We will study these in some depth later on in the book.

Keep it to yourself

Feng shui is currently enjoying a massive amount of interest and use in the West, and quite rightly so as it is a valuable tool in living in harmony with ourselves. However, it is just that – a tool. It is not a spiritual path or a way of scoring points off your neighbours or friends. It's something that almost needs to be carried out in private – you do it and make the changes and it benefits your life but there's no need to let anyone else know. It is also unforgivable to comment on the feng shui of someone else's dwelling. If they know you know something about feng shui and they want your opinion they will ask – if they don't then you shouldn't volunteer it. What works for someone may well not work for another person. Feng shui doesn't work in isolation, it's very dependent on the people involved. There's no such thing as bad feng shui – merely feng shui that doesn't work for a particular person living in a particular place. I have a friend who lives in a house that has what I would consider to be appalling feng shui and yet he thrives there. That's because the particular make-up he has in his personality allows him to not only cope with the feng shui but to actually benefit from it enormously – and who am I to say he is wrong? Keep it to yourself. Feng shui is not enhanced by fundamentalism or a born-again approach. It is a subtle skill and it is enjoyed and propagated in a subtle manner.

Feng shui and dancing

Feng shui is an exact skill but it is also subject to an enormous amount of personal interpretation precisely because it needs the personal input so much. Having studied feng shui myself for the past 20 years I'm still surprised when I hear that it can be summed up as 'keep your toilet lid closed, no beams over the bed and hang a wind chime over the front door'. Nothing could be further from the truth. These things may well be true, but feng shui is more; it's about a subtle interplay with energy, about ourselves and how we choose to live, and about learning to be part of a personal solution rather than being part of the problem. Chu Lin, a Taoist teacher and Ch'i Master, says that 'life is learning to dance with the energy of the Infinite, feng shui is the steps of that dance'. In this book we will map out some of those steps and the dance can begin.

Which dance will we do?

Just as there is a difference between a waltz and a tango so there is a difference between the various schools of feng shui – of which there are three basic ones. The edges of these three schools of feng shui have become blurred and they overlap in many places but they can be summed up as:

☻ **Compass or lo p'an feng shui**. This relies heavily on the use of a traditional feng shui compass, called a *lo p'an*, with up to 64 rings of information which a feng shui consultant will use to determine whether your house is right for you. Compass feng shui is traditional in China as a service provided for burial. The Chinese are very superstitious and believe that a person buried in a 'wrong' place will return to haunt the living – a hungry ghost – and that it is essential to make sure the grave is aligned correctly.

- **Directional or Pah Kwa feng shui**. This is feng shui that uses the direction your house faces to arrive at information as well as dividing your house up into eight areas or enrichments – the *Pah Kwa* (sometimes spelt *bagua*) – that govern every area of your life such as relationships, family, career and health.
- **Intuitive or yin yang feng shui**. This branch of feng shui is more concerned with the way energy flows in and around your home and how you fit in with that energy.

We will cover all three schools of thought but, as we don't all have access to a traditional feng shui compass, the first will be dealt with only generally. Directional feng shui is very formal and can become confusing if your home doesn't fit exactly into a Pah Kwa shape but it is a useful way of learning feng shui to begin with. Yin yang feng shui, which is the one we will work with mainly, is instinctive and intuitive and allows you a greater input and greater control. But our edges will be blurred and we will use all three in different ways.

Chinese spelling

For many years here in the West we have used a system of Chinese spelling called the 'Wade Giles' system. This gave us such names as Peking. There is now, however, a new system called 'pinyin' which gives us Beijing instead of Peking. It also makes ch'i become qi. While I am happy with Beijing, I cannot find it in my heart to use qi – therefore I have used ch'i throughout the book. It also explains why there may be differences in spelling of such things as Pah Kwa (bagua). And the oldest classic of all – the *I Ching* – becomes the Yi Jing. Luckily feng shui remains as feng shui. These things can play havoc with the spell-checker on a word processor.

Other points

Two things – one, the Chinese always put south at the top on compasses. Because I have grown used to this I will also do this throughout the book. It may seem strange at first but you will quickly get used to it, especially when you realise how much importance the Chinese place on the south as an auspicious direction – and why not, it certainly is sunnier and happier than always looking north.

Second, when we get to the bit about trigrams and compass directions I use the Early Heaven Sequence not the Later Heaven Sequence. I shall explain. The Early Heaven Sequence of trigrams was originally evolved for use in feng shui. It is a logical and rational way of laying out the compass directions with yin and yang opposite each other at the north and south respectively, as well as polarities opposite each other and wind opposite thunder, mountain opposite lake, water opposite fire and heaven opposite earth – it all makes sense and fits together perfectly, as you will see later.

The Later Heaven Sequence was evolved for use with the *I Ching*, the ancient Chinese oracle, The Book of Changes. While the two do go hand in hand in many respects, the sequences do not. The Later Heaven Sequence doesn't make much sense for feng shui purposes, although I am aware that many feng shui practitioners use it and I wouldn't want to upset any of them by saying it is wrong – it's just that I can't work with it. The early, or former, sequence dates back to around 3000 BCE (Before Common Era) when it was formulated by the Chinese emperor, Fu Hsi, who is said to have found the sequence marked on the back of a tortoise he encountered on a bank of the Yellow River. The Later Heaven Sequence was modified by King Wen around 1000 BCE, although no satisfactory explanation has been given as to why the new order was suggested – it's still a mystery. The funny thing is that if you look at any traditional lo p'an (feng shui compass) it is invariably marked with the early sequence but the feng shui consultant may well be laying out his or her Pah Kwa in the later sequence. As I say, I can't work with the later sequence but I will explain it and its order in the relevant chapter. Perhaps we'd better get on with it.

1

THE HISTORY OF FENG SHUI

Into my heart an air that kills
From yon far country blows:
What are those blue remembered hills,
What spires, what farms are those?
That is the land of lost content,
I see it shining plain,
The happy highways where I went
And cannot come again.

A. E. HOUSMAN

It may seem strange to think that feng shui has a history but it does. And it's a history that takes into account many inventions and developments both in China and the rest of the world. A study of feng shui and its lengthy history would occupy not only the whole of this book but many other books as well, so I have tried to pick some interesting and relevant topics to give you an idea of how interconnected feng shui is with everything else that goes on around us. It's also a way to get you thinking in the same vein as all the students of feng shui who have gone before.

I will begin with printing, which you may think has no connection with feng shui, but when you consider that nearly every home in China has an almanac which, for them, is an essential part of feng shui, you will realise that without the invention of printing feng shui could neither have spread as widely as it has nor been so accessible or popular.

EARLY CHINESE INVENTIONS
AND DISCOVERIES

In the West we have a particular view of world history that often tends to overlook or neglect developments that happened in China. For instance, we know that the printing press was invented in Germany around 1448 by Johann Gutenburg, and that by 1500 there were printing presses in 14 European countries. But did you also know that the Chinese had mastered printing a lot earlier? The world's oldest surviving book printed on paper is the *Diamond Sutra* discovered by Sir Aurel Stein at Tunhuang in 1907. It is a book printed in 868 that translates the complete text of a Sanskrit work into Chinese, with a very elaborate frontispiece of the Buddha in discourse with his disciple Subhuti. And there were even earlier works dating from around 700 that don't survive in their entirety. The print runs of some of these books was fantastic: an early Buddhist sutra was printed in a run of 1 million copies.

Francis Bacon, the seventeenth-century philosopher, suggested that three inventions marked civilisation's turning point – the printing press, gunpowder and the magnetic compass. We've looked at the printing press but what about the other two? Well, gunpowder was used in China as early as 850 CE (Common Era) and it wasn't used in the West until some three centuries later. Gunpowder wasn't invented in China as a form of warfare, although that's certainly what it was to become, but merely as a by-product of the Taoist's search for immortality. The Taoists were early alchemists who, when investigating the properties of saltpetre, discovered that by mixing saltpetre with other constituents, such as sulphur, you could get it to burn fiercely – even explode. The first mention of such properties of saltpetre in the West was in an Arabic book in 1240 CE where it is described as 'Chinese snow'.

The magnetic compass

The third of the inventions mentioned by Francis Bacon was the magnetic compass. The first reference in European literature to a compass is from the *De Naturis Rerum*, written in 1190 CE by Alexander Neckham:

> *The sailors, when they are ignorant to what point the ship's course is directed, touch the magnet with a needle. This then whirls in a circle until, when its motion ceases, its point looks direct to the North.*

It would seem that the Europeans got the idea of the compass from the Chinese who had been using it as early as the fourth century BCE, when the first mention of a lodestone compass is made in the *Book of the Devil Valley Masters*. The author is not known but may well have been the philosopher Su Ch'in. He wrote:

> *When the people of Cheng go out to collect jade, they carry a South-pointer with them so as not to lose their way.*

And Shen Kua wrote in his *Dream Pool Essays*:

> *Magicians rub the point of a needle with the lodestone; then it is able to point to the South. It may be balanced on the rim of a cup where it can be made to turn more easily but it is best to suspend it by a single cocoon fibre of new silk attached to the centre of the needle by a piece of wax the size of a mustard seed – then, hanging in a windless place, it will always point to the South.*

Compass needles

The early Chinese compass needles were usually made in the shape of a small fish and were always aligned to point south rather than north. They were set on boards which had the points of a compass laid out as well as the symbols from the *I Ching*. These boards, not unlike a traditional feng shui compass, also had inset rings showing the magnetic variation of the poles so that they were very accurate. The boards were used by map makers, travellers and sailors. They were also used by Taoist priests for geomantic purposes; aligning grave sites, houses, temples, and even entire cities.

The fact that the Chinese had compasses as early and as accurate as they did also gives us evidence that they knew about steel making, thermo-remanence, cartography and astronomy. They were a civilisation reaching its peak while European civilisation was still in its infancy.

The Earth's magnetic field

The Chinese also had quite a detailed knowledge of the Earth's magnetic field, something Europe wasn't to acquire until 1600, and they believed, quite rightly, that the Earth's field was an active force. This active force was capable of exerting change and being measured. The Chinese saw a close relationship between magnetic energy and ch'i, or cosmic energy. They believed that ch'i flows along magnetic lines and needs to be nurtured and encouraged, and that to block or oppose the flow of ch'i can only lead to ill health and bad luck.

CH'I

The concept of ch'i was fundamental to the Chinese understanding of life, nature, the cosmos and humanity. Ch'i is in everything, and is a living force. Everything and everyone has its own particular ch'i. There is even group ch'i which is capable of giving off a resonance. Armies were seen as having their distinct ch'i which could be seen by certain Taoist priests as hanging or hovering over the heads of the soldiers as they marched into battle. Some armies had good ch'i and others bad ch'i.

An army's ch'i

To detect the nature of an army's ch'i, a musical priest
would blow on special pitch pipes and from the tone
deduce what sort of ch'i the army had and thus make a
pronouncement about whether battle should be delayed or
indulged in at once and how successful the army might be.

Earth sounds

That ch'i was capable of being tested by the quality of
sound of a pipe being played was taken further. Each
month was believed to have its own particular pitch of
sound: there being 12 months thus there were 12 notes to
the year.

These 12 special notes or tones were terribly important, and
the ancient Chinese were concerned that the tones may
become corrupted by natural forces, wars, civil
disturbances, even moral decline. These 12 tones had to be
tested every year to be certain that they retained their
clarity; if they did not then action could be taken to remedy
them. This testing of the monthly sounds of the Earth was a
bizarre and elaborate ritual that took place in China for at
least 1,700 years, from the first century BCE (at least) up to
the sixteenth century CE when it was abandoned.

Hermetically sealed laboratories

To test the Earth sounds a tent with a series of enclosed
corridors was erected so that you would have to keep
walking the entire length of the tent before you could enter
the next partition. By the time you reached the centre you
had, to all intents and purposes, entered a hermetically
sealed laboratory, not unlike a photographic darkroom. No
breath of air from the outside could penetrate the inner
portion of the tent. In the very centre, 12 pitch pipes would
be set up and their correct lengths verified. This was to
confirm the pitches emitted by the pipes, which formed the

basis for all measurements. By the first century BCE the procedure known as 'observing the ch'i' or 'the blowing of the ashes' was instituted:

> *The ch'i of heaven and earth combine and produce wind. The ch'i associated with wind being correct, the ch'i for each of the twelve months causes a sympathetic reaction in the pitch pipes. All the pipes being arranged round the compass points in their proper corresponding positions. The upper ends of the pitch pipes are stuffed with the ashes of reeds, and a watch kept upon them according to the calendar. When the emanation [ch'i] for a given month arrives, the ashes of the appropriate pitch pipe fly out and the tube is cleared.*

TS'AI YUNG (c. 178 CE)

Again it should be stressed that this ritual went on every month of every year for at least 1,700 years.

THE KNOWLEDGE OF ENERGY MOVEMENT

The Chinese are an older, wiser civilisation than we may ever realise. Their knowledge of the way energy moves and flows is very ancient – and it is knowledge that is becoming increasingly available in the West – knowledge that can help us to lead improved, healthier and happier lives. This knowledge of energy movement is known as feng shui. The Chinese believed that energy moves in the same way as wind and water does – and that's exactly what feng shui means – wind and water.

The Chinese have had what we would recognise and call a civilisation for around 3,000 years. During that time their population has risen from around 58 million (the census of 2 CE, Han dynasty) to 1,132 million in 1990. That's an awful lot of lives lived – and each life lived has been useful in discovering more about how human beings are affected by where and how they live. When you study the fundamental approach of Taoism, which is the ancient and traditional religion of China, that there is only the 'now' to be considered it makes sense to make that now supremely comfortable and enjoyable. Perhaps as people in the West increasingly turn away from organised religions and seek a more personal approach they discover that Taoism has a lot to offer – and with Taoism comes feng shui – the making of the living in the moment more accessible. The Christian religions have their view of a future heavenly reward; the Hindus have countless gods and goddesses to be appeased; the Buddhists have a Nirvana to be striven for, or at least the chance of reincarnation. But for the Taoists there is only this life and the chance of happiness is now.

Everything about feng shui is about making changes to our lives to improve them now; to make them more comfortable, to increase our wealth and health, to make sure our relationships work well and provide us with satisfaction, to provide comfort and nurture for our loved ones and families. Feng shui is not about building up spiritual merit or investing in any future existence. It is purely and simply about using the resources around us to best effect. And it has been in operation basically in the form in which we find it today for at least 2,000 years.

Early feng shui consultants

We even know who the earliest feng shui consultants were owing to the richness of written texts from China. For instance, one of the best known and most popular or successful was Chao Ta who lived around 221–65 CE. He is accredited with inventing the first feng shui compass which was marked with not only compass directions but also the 64 hexagrams of the *I Ching*, the 5 elements, the 12 animals and the 28 lunar mansions.

2

YIN AND YANG AND
THE FIVE ELEMENTS

Beautiful must be the mountains whence ye come,
And bright in the fruitful valleys the streams,
Where from ye learn your song:
Where are those starry woods? O might I wander there,
Among the flowers, which in that heavenly air
Bloom the year long!

ROBERT BRIDGES

If you have previously visited and explored the strange country of Taoist philosophy, please excuse me if I am going over old ground with you. If, however, you have never before ventured here then I will take it slowly and explain it all clearly and simply.

UNDERSTANDING TAOISM

To understand feng shui we have to understand Taoism. To understand Taoism we have to go back to before the beginning of time. Then there was nothing except infinite space – the cosmos. This is known to the Taoists as the blue-bag, a sort of affectionate nickname (its correct name by the way is the *T'ai Ch'i* – the Supreme Ultimate). Out of this infinite space came two fundamental principles that govern everything – matter and spirit. Matter is known as yin, and is seen as dark and solid. Spirit is known as yang, and is seen as light and ethereal. The two became the yin/yang symbol which formed a perfect circle – the T'ai Ch'i (see Figure 2.1).

Figure 2.1 Yin/yang symbol

THE QUALITIES OF YIN AND YANG

You will notice that each section, whether light or dark, has a tiny dot of its opposite within it. That is because the Taoists believe that nothing is completely one or the other – there must always be the seed of the other already buried in it and ready to grow. Yin and yang are not static but always changing, moving to their opposite. If yin is death and yang is life then we are continually moving between the two. If yin is night and yang is day then we are constantly changing from one to the other.

Yin is sometimes expressed as the feminine principle while yang is said to be the male principle. Remember, though, that they are always changing from one to the other so nothing is ever 'female' or 'male', but merely reflecting a dominant principle at that time – expressing its yin-ness or yang-ness for that moment.

Listed opposite are some of the qualities or principles of yin and yang.

yin	yang
creation	heaven
earth	sky
negative	positive
passive	active
female	male
receptive	creative
down	up
north	south
matter	spirit
dark	light
night	day
cold	heat
soft	hard
wet	dry
winter	summer
shadow	sunshine

Yin and yang and disease

This list is by no means exhaustive. For example, Chinese herbal practitioners and acupuncturists will classify diseases and ailments according to their yin or yang qualities as well as classifying both the human body and its internal organs.

yin	yang
The disease	
chronic	acute
non-active	virulent
moist	dry
retiring	advancing
lingering	hasty
weak	powerful
decaying	flourishing
patient feels cold	patient feels hot
skin cold to touch	skin hot to touch
low temperature	high temperature
shivering	feverish

yin	yang
The body	
interior	surface
abdomen	back
chest	spine
blood	ch'i energy
cloudy body fluids	clear body fluids

When we consider the feng shui of health we must also bear some of these qualities in mind.

Yin and yang and compass directions

The yin/yang symbol should always be shown with the yin to the right. This reflects compass directions. The light yang is at the top representing summer and the south, while the dark yin is at the bottom representing winter and the north. Chinese compasses are the opposite way round to those in the West: they have their south at the top where our north would be, and their west to the right and east to the left (see Figure 2.2).

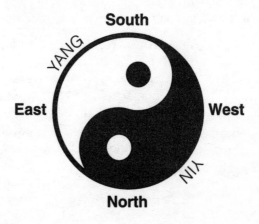

Figure 2.2 Yin/yang with compass directions

Yin and yang and the human body

The yin/yang symbol also represents the human body – the head at the top representing spirit, yang, and the body below representing matter, yin. Yang, male, is the left-hand side of the body, while the right-hand side is yin, female (see Figure 2.3). Much research is being carried out in the West into the two brain halves: the left brain controls the right side and would seem also to govern the more intuitive, artistic side of our nature, and is known as the female brain; the right brain controls the left side and governs our more mathematical thought processes, and is known as the male brain. It is interesting that Western science is just discovering this; it seems the Chinese knew it 5,000 years ago.

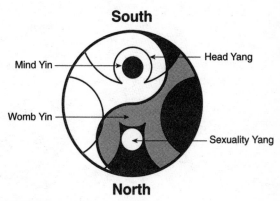

Figure 2.3 Yin/yang with human body

Illness can be seen as a result of an imbalance of yin and yang. The beginning of life originates from yin/yang. Yin grows from yang, yang grows from yin and neither can exist without the other.

The abilities of the human body are seen as yang, while food, the energy source, is seen as yin. The body depends on the food for life, and yet to obtain the energy from the food it must be acted upon by the digestive system of the body.

Once we understand how an imbalance of yin and yang affects our bodies and our health we can begin to see how feng shui fits in with health – and health is an important part of feng shui. Get the balance wrong and our health suffers. Get the balance right and our health benefits.

YIN AND YANG AND THE TRIGRAMS

As a sort of shorthand the Taoists ascribed a single unbroken line to yang and a single broken line to represent yin (see Figure 2.4).

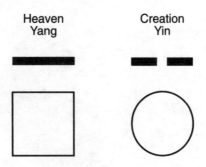

Figure 2.4 The two lines

Using the yin, north, and yang, south, we can combine these two symbols to create another two to represent east and west, spring and autumn.

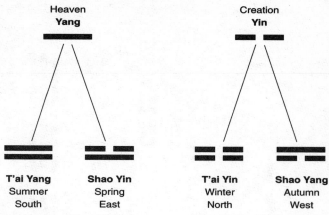

Figure 2.5 The four lines

South is known as *T'ai Yang* or Great Yang, while west is known as *Shao Yang* or Lesser Yang. North is *T'ai Yin*, Great Yin, and east is *Shao Yin*, Lesser Yin (see Figure 2.5).

The eight trigrams

From these four new symbols we can then produce another four to give us the rest of the compass and the mid-season points (see Figure 2.6).

These are known as the eight trigrams (a trigram is three parallel lines).

- ☻ The top lines represent the duality of heaven and creation – the yin/yang.
- ☻ The middle lines represent heaven and creation coming together to create the four seasons and the cardinal points of the compass.
- ☻ The bottom lines represent us, people.

The eight trigrams are all named and have various significance and attributes. They are listed on page 25 along with their Chinese name and its translation, their seasons, direction and main attributes.

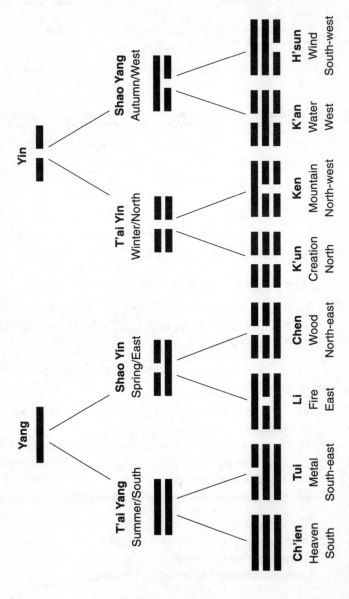

Figure 2.6 The eight trigrams

- **Ch'ien** – *The Creative*, heaven, south, summer
- **Tui** – *The Lake*, metal, south-east, joy
- **Li** – *The Clinging*, fire, east, spring, the sun
- **Chen** – *The Arousing*, wood, north-east, thunder
- **K'un** – *The Receptive*, creation, north, winter
- **Ken** – *The Stillness*, mountain, north-west, calm
- **K'an** – *The Dangerous*, water, west, autumn, the moon
- **H'sun** – *The Gentle*, wind, south-west, wood

We can now form these trigrams into an octagon to give us the compass and the seasons (see Figure 2.7).

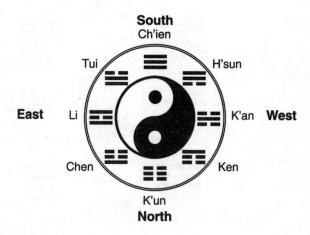

Figure 2.7 The Pah Kwa, the Great Symbol (Former Heaven Sequence)

This is known as the Pah Kwa, the Great Symbol, and is a very lucky symbol for the Chinese representing as it does almost their entire spiritual and philosophical beliefs in one image.

You will notice that south is at the top, as is correct for a Chinese compass, and north at the bottom.

The eight trigrams are thought to have been developed by Fu Hsi, a Chinese emperor, around 3000 BCE. It is said that he found the eight trigrams in the ornate markings on the shell of a tortoise which he studied on the banks of the Yellow River. The sequence in which he found them is known as the Former Heaven Sequence. Around 1000 BCE they were rearranged into a different sequence called the Later Heaven Sequence by King Wen, a philosopher and founder of the Chou Dynasty (see Figure 2.8).

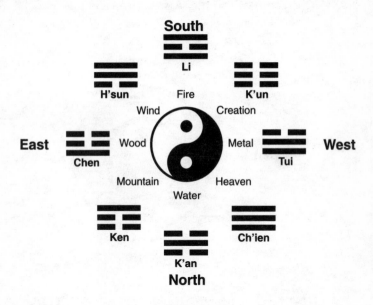

Figure 2.8 The Later Heaven Sequence

THE *I CHING*

These eight trigrams can be paired into 64 new symbols (8 multiplied by 8) called hexagrams which use six lines. These 64 hexagrams each have a meaning; Fu Hsi ascribed them first as a herbal and agricultural almanac which he called the *I Ching* (pronounced *ee ching*), the Book of Changes. As this was more than 5,000 years ago the *I Ching* is probably the oldest book in existence and it has remained virtually unchanged to the present day. The only major restructuring was done by King Wen who added to Fu Hsi's interpretations and changed, for some strange reason, the order of the trigrams as we saw in the Introduction. If you turn to Chapter 9 you can see how the order changes for *I Ching* readings for your home – room by room.

THE FIVE ELEMENTS

The yin yang symbol also incorporates into its design five elements:

- South–south-east – **fire**
- East–north-east – **wood**
- North-east–north – **water**
- North-west–west – **metal**
- West–south-west – **earth**

You will notice that two of these elements come completely under the auspices of yin – metal and water – and two under yang – fire and wood. Metal is known as the lesser yin; water as the greater yin. Wood is the lesser yang; fire the greater yang. Metal is known as the face of beauty, water as the giver of life. Wood and fire are known as the eyes and ears of the universe respectively. Earth is both yin and yang, and for that reason is often shown as occupying the centre of the yin yang symbol, but for the purposes of feng shui is shown between fire and metal.

There is obviously some overlap of the elements with the compass directions, there being eight directions but only five elements. It's probably best shown as a diagram (see Figure 2.9).

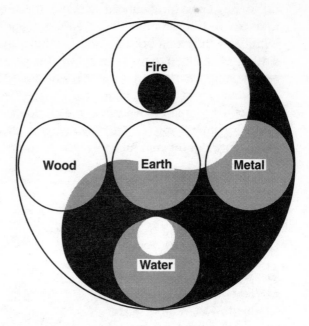

Figure 2.9 The five elements with yin/yang symbol

The Theory of the Five Aspects (Wu Hsing)

Most Oriental wisdom, medicine and philosophy is based on the Theory of the Five Aspects (Wu Hsing) which suggests that, while we are a combination of all of the elements or aspects, we do tend to display predominantly the characteristics of one over the others. These elements are not the elements of conventional Western astrology. It is better to regard them more as aspects of character.

- **Earth** – *T'u* – The Diplomat – moderate, sense of loyalty, harmonious, likes to belong, pays attention to detail, likes company, needs to be needed, can be stubborn, should avoid damp.
- **Fire** – *Huo* – The Magician – compassionate, intuitive, communicative, likes pleasure, seeks excitement, likes

to be in love, doesn't like to be bored, should avoid heat.

- ☺ **Water** – *Shui* – The Philosopher – imaginative, honest, clever, seeks knowledge, original, tough, independent, can be secretive, needs to be protected, should avoid cold.
- ☺ **Metal** – *Chin* – The Catalyst – organised, likes to control, precise, discriminating, needs to be right, likes order and cleanliness, appreciates quality, should avoid dryness.
- ☺ **Wood** – *Mu* – The Pioneer – expansive, purposeful, active, likes to be busy, can be domineering, needs to win, practical, should avoid windy places to live.

Knowing which element you are will be helpful in your understanding of feng shui. This you can determine from asking yourself questions such as: Which season do I feel best in? What colour do I like best? Which illnesses am I prone to? Which facial feature would I consider dominant in myself? Which description of the five elemental types best describes me? If you go to a Chinese acupuncturist he or she will ask a lot more questions and also look at your tongue, smell you, check your pulses and use numerous other techniques to ascertain your element – but then you would be treated on that particular element's meridians and the acupuncturist needs to be very exact.

You can probably gauge which element you are from the descriptions. The magician: Is that you? Or how about the diplomat? Would that best describe you? Quite a good way of doing this is to ask your friends to sum you up – they may be a little more objective than you will be about yourself. You might even be able to tell just from listening to your intuition.

Traditionally, the feng shui practitioner would have determined which element you were, and whether you were yin or yang, from the year of your birth. These dominant elements change with the years and are regarded as yin or yang. What year were you born? What is the last number? For example, if you were born in a year ending in 0 you are yang metal. Here is a full list:

Year ending	Yin/yang	Element
1	yin	metal
2	yang	water
3	yin	water
4	yang	wood
5	yin	wood
6	yang	fire
7	yin	fire
8	yang	earth
9	yin	earth

This may fit in with what you intuitively feel is the right element for you. If the year seems 'wrong' then go with what you *feel* to be right. (See Appendix II for a full list of these years. The Chinese year doesn't change exactly as the Western year does – and it varies each year.)

If you want to know whether you are yin or yang then it's probably easiest just to ask yourself what you do for a living. Yang types are out in the world; yin types tend to make their living from home. Yang types like mixing with other people; yin types are more solitary. Yang types like new projects, new ideas and starting things off. Yin types are more methodical, better at completing projects and paying much more attention to detail. Yang types are noisier, more boisterous, bolder and quicker. Yin types are quieter, more 'laid-back', more thoughtful and considerate. Do you know which you are yet?

Obviously, whether you are a yin or yang type of element will affect you. Yang types like darker, cooler houses while yin types tend to prefer lighter more spacious accommodation. Because yin is dark it seeks the light. Because yang is light it seeks the dark. It is the same with the elements.

- **Fire**: the south, the expansive, seeks the cool of the north
- **Water**: the north, the nurturer, seeks the heat of the south
- **Wood**: the east, the clinging, the wisdom, seeks the unpredictability of the west
- **Metal**: the west, the changeable, seeks the wisdom and calmness of the east
- **Earth**: the south-west, the calming, soothing, gentle wind seeks the thunder and arousal of the north-east.

You can see now why two people sharing the same home may well have two very differing decorating styles, so knowing which element they are can be helpful. As well as the elements, each of the four compass directions is also represented by symbols:

- **South** – the sun representing the creative
- **North** – the moon representing the receptive
- **East** – a mountain representing stillness
- **West** – a lake representing the hidden and the unknown.

Each of the different elements has contrasting responses to the others:

- **Earth**: helps metal, is helped by fire; hinders water, is hindered by wood.
- **Fire**: helps earth, is helped by wood; hinders metal, is hindered by water.
- **Water**: helps wood, is helped by metal; hinders fire, is hindered by earth.
- **Metal**: helps water, is helped by earth; hinders wood, is hindered by fire.
- **Wood**: helps fire, is helped by water; hinders earth, is hindered by metal.

Each of these five elements rules or influences different internal organs, parts of the body, emotional expressions, colours, tastes and energies. They are also indicative of very different types of people.

Element	wood	fire	earth	metal	water
Direction	east	south	south-west	west	north
Colour	green	red	yellow	white	black
Season	spring	summer	late summer	autumn	winter
Internal organs	liver	heart	spleen	lungs	kidneys
	gall bladder	small intestine	stomach	large intestine	bladder
Facial features*	eyes	tongue	mouth	nose	ears
Body*	tendons	pulse	muscle	skin/hair	bones
Expression	anger	gaiety	pensiveness	sorrow	fright
Taste	sour	bitter	sweet	pungent	salt
Energy	wind	hot	wet	dry	cold
Smell**	rancid	scorched	fragrant	putrid	rotten

* These are the parts most prone to ailments

**The names for the smells may have lost a little in their translation

The five elements and types of homes

These five elements not only relate to the types of people but also to the types of homes and what is in them. Obviously, a timber-clad dwelling will be predominantly wood; a brick-built flat will be earth; a house built over a river, water; an apartment made from steel girders will be metal; and a home brightly lit with many lights will reflect the element of fire. Too much of one element will display an imbalance and will need to be modified. Similarly, someone who is one particular type of element may well live in a home that is predominantly another element and that will throw them out of balance. We will see how to correct this in later chapters.

THE FIVE SENTIMENTS

These five elemental types, known as the Five Phase Theory, are further categorised into the Harmony of the Five Sentiments, these being anger, joy, fear, sorrow, and pensiveness giving a total of a basic 25 combinations. To keep the body healthy it is necessary to keep these sentiments in balance. While these sentiments have their 'ideal' in a particular element, they are experienced by all elemental types. For instance, anger is typical of wood types but it could be that a metal element could also experience anger as the dominant sentiment, whereas a wood element may experience joy as the dominant sentiment.

The Harmony of the Five Sentiments

Although, traditionally, each of these sentiments belongs to a particular element, you may well find that the description of a sentiment that best fits you belongs to an element other than yours. This could mean that, although you are predominantly one thing you may be expressing it as something else. This can lead to someone feeling as if they were somehow in the 'wrong' situation in life. It may mean that the location isn't ideal and it is affecting the expression of a particular sentiment. Feng shui is a way of getting us to look at our sentiment and making sure it 'matches' the element. Sometimes when we are in a particularly unhappy relationship we express the 'wrong' sentiment. As soon as we leave the relationship the balance is restored and we again revert to the 'correct' sentiment. Sometimes a separation isn't necessary – by merely doing some work on the relationship we can free up energy that has been stuck and improve our situation.

- 😔 **Anger**. If the emotion of anger dominates then you will be easily upset by frustrations, prone to give in to violent outbursts, be volatile and unpredictable. Seen by others as self-controlled and self-disciplined, when stress and tension build up you can explode into rage. Positive qualities are that you get things done, and you are brilliant at new projects and at motivating other people. Illnesses that you are prone to are ulcers, migraines and haemorrhoids. Yang wood types tend to externalise anger; yin wood internalise anger. Key word is **magnanimity**.

Joy. When joy is the main motivating force in your life you are liable to suffer extreme mood swings: you're either up or down, never in between. You can become an endless 'pleasure seeker'. You crave excitement and feel empty and alone without it. Your positive qualities are that you are great fun to be around – others are never bored when around a fire/joy person although you might wear them out with your energy. You have the ability to transform any situation to one of adventure and excitement. Illness can run to anorexia, schizophrenia, manic-depressive psychosis or hypoglycaemia. Yang fire types tend to be manic while yin fire types can be depressive. Key word is **purpose**.

Fear. If you live your life with fear you can become isolated, hermit-like, even withdrawn. You anticipate the worst, imagine the worst-case scenario in everything you do. You cut yourself off from the world believing it to be a fundamentally evil place which is out to harm you. Your positive qualities are that you are intensely nurturing and make a good parent and teacher. Illnesses can run to deafness, arthritis and senility. Yang water types will be fearful of external stimuli while yin water will be subject to internal fears. Key word is **insight**.

Sorrow. If sorrow predominates, you will isolate yourself from excitement or any emotional activity to protect yourself from the emotion you fear most: sorrow. You believe that is what you deserve and subsequently shut off from the world of relationships.

You like to control everyone around you so no one can hurt you. Your positive quality is that you are extremely sensitive to others' needs and will make yourself of use to the rest of humanity to prevent it suffering too much – you make a great healer. Illnesses manifest as constipation, frigidity and asthma. Yang metal will be sad about external stimuli while yin metal will be sad about the past. Key word is **order**.

☻ **Pensiveness**. You basically worry over little details to the point of obsession. You get bogged down in minutiae. You like security and safety and can become lethargic and apathetic when faced with new challenges mainly because it is all too much for you. Your positive qualities are that you are extremely logical and precise, making you a good diplomat and counsellor – you can see the wood for the trees. Illnesses tend to show up as obesity, poor digestion, heart problems and high blood pressure. Yang earth types will think long and hard about external detail while yin earth types will worry about internal minutiae. Key word is **honesty**.

Which category do you feel you belong in? The more we know about ourselves the easier feng shui becomes. If we don't know ourselves then how can we effect change in our lives?

FENG SHUI AND CHINESE ASTROLOGY

In China feng shui relies as heavily on Chinese astrology – the 12 animals – as it does on compass directions. You'll probably know which animal you are but did you know each animal also has an element? You know which element belongs to the year you were born (see Appendix II) but you also have an element that belongs to your animal – a secret side to you known as your natural element. The elements for the 12 animals are:

- Water (north) – pig, rat and ox
- Metal (west) – dog, cockerel and monkey
- Fire (south) – goat, horse and snake
- Wood (east) – tiger, cat and dragon

Earth occupies the centre of the compass. If your year element and natural element are the same it reinforces your element. But if they are different you may need to decide which one dominates.

- **Fire**   Ideal house – north-facing, comfortable, warm house but quite grand, like a manor house. Good interior colours – reds, oranges. Key word is **enthusiasm**.
- **Water**   Ideal house – south-facing, older more traditional house, like a period thatched cottage. Good interior colours – black, dark blues. Key word is **hope**.
- **Wood**   Ideal house – west-facing, unusual, distinctive or individual like a lighthouse. Good interior colours – green, gold. Key word is **confronting**.
- **Metal**   Ideal house – east-facing, modern, designer house. Good interior colours – white, grey, pale blues. Key word is **organisation**.
- **Earth**   Ideal house – a mid-terrace would be perfect or a basement flat but it would have to be family oriented – perhaps a farmhouse. Good interior colours – yellow, pale green and brown, dark grey. Key word is **caring**.

Here's an example of how to tie the two types of elements together. Suppose you are metal (from your year) and water (from your animal). Ideally you may go for a period home (water) but it would be ordered and neat (metal). Or perhaps you are fire (year) and wood (animal). You may go for a manor house (fire) but decorate it completely in modern furniture (wood) which would be unusual.

In Chapter 3 we will look at how the concept of energy interacts with yin and yang, and how the eight compass points are important to feng shui.

3

CH'I AND THE EIGHT COMPASS POINTS

I live not in myself, but I become
Portion of that around me; and to me
High mountains are a feeling, but the hum
Of human cities torture.

BYRON

CH'I

Yin and yang, the compass directions and the five elements
are the building blocks of feng shui but we need a glue;
something to bind them all together – and that is ch'i. The
Taoists see ch'i as the universal energy of life. It is never
static but always on the move, flowing from yin to yang,
from yang to yin. Its Japanese equivalent is *Ki*, and its Indian
counterpart is *prana* or universal breath. Ch'i has no form
but permeates everything. Without ch'i to give us life we
are dead. It nourishes us and profoundly affects not only
our moods but our health, relationships and luck.

How ch'i flows

Ch'i flows harmoniously between the two polarities of yin
and yang unless it is interrupted or hindered. Ch'i that is
allowed to stagnate or become corrupted is known as *sha*,
which actually means 'obnoxious vapours' and will bring us
ill health, bad luck and poor relationships. Sha impoverishes
us while ch'i enriches us. Like yin and yang, ch'i and sha are
always moving towards and away from each other. Ch'i

cannot be neglected or it becomes sha – it has to be helped, nurtured and encouraged. Sha, on the other hand, left to its own devices rarely becomes ch'i, while it is still passing through your home, but merely disintegrates further. To encourage sha to return to health you have to take positive and direct action – feng shui.

There are various forms that ch'i takes, especially the ch'i of the human body. Within the body ch'i is categorised into four types:

- **Original ch'i**   Sometimes known as real or correct ch'i and it represents the strengths and weaknesses of the body in combating all forms of illness. If the original ch'i is weak, infection can take place: restoring original ch'i will ward off illness.

- **Internal organ ch'i**   This is the specific energy of particular organs: there is ch'i of the liver, ch'i of the heart, ch'i of the lungs, and so on.

  The combined ch'i of the stomach and spleen is known as central ch'i. If this becomes weakened it causes difficulties in the function of the digestive system, a slowing down in the rate of mental activity, weak voice and problems with the uterus. These conditions must be treated by a method which strengthens central ch'i.

  The ch'i of the lungs and heart together is known as ancestral ch'i and assists respiration and circulation. If the ancestral ch'i is weakened it causes a weak heartbeat and problems with breathing.

- **Guarding ch'i**   This surrounds all the meridians and is dispersed throughout the whole body. It travels outside the meridians and is regarded as the boundary fence of all internal systems.

- **Protein ch'i**   This ch'i travels within the pulse meridians and provides vital protein to the blood, and it can be seen that guarding ch'i and protein ch'i work very closely together: the outer and the inner.

The disruption of ch'i

Ch'i can be disrupted in one of three ways:

☯ **Weakening ch'i** This means that there is insufficient energy. This is most commonly noticeable when the ch'i of the lungs and the spleen are weakened. The symptoms of this are a loss of appetite, reluctance to speak, sweating for no apparent reason, dizzy spells and a feeble pulse.

☯ **Stagnation of ch'i** This occurs when the mechanism of internal organ functioning meets an obstruction to its normal operation and is found mainly in the spleen, lungs and liver. Stagnation of ch'i in the lungs results in tightness of the chest, pain, wheezy breathing and too much phlegm. Symptoms can include a tightness in the chest, sides and abdomen accompanied by pain.

Ch'i stagnating in the liver produces a bloated abdomen, abdominal pain, and in women a painful menstrual cycle with irregular periods.

Stagnant spleen ch'i produces indigestion and a painful swollen abdomen.

Stagnation of ch'i in the meridian veins will result in aching in the muscles and joints of all of the limbs, sometimes with some swelling.

☯ **Mischannelling of ch'i** This takes place when the ch'i flows in the wrong direction. Each organ's ch'i flows in a particular direction. The stomach and lung ch'i flows downwards, and if either flows upwards then illness can result. For example: downward-flowing lung ch'i being reversed would cause asthma and coughs whereas downward-flowing stomach ch'i being reversed would cause vomiting and nausea. Reversed liver ch'i would cause vomiting of blood, fainting and unconsciousness.

Blood

Whereas ch'i is seen as yang, blood is seen as yin: the two providing a nourishing balance and complementing each other. They are both equally necessary for a healthy body. An old Chinese saying is: 'Blood gives birth to ch'i, but ch'i rules the blood'.

The motivating energy of ch'i encourages the blood to flow. If the ch'i stagnates, the blood clots. If there is an inadequate supply of blood, a loss of sensitivity and even paralysis can result.

In the West we might be inclined to regard ch'i as merely a single Chinese concept; in reality it is a vast and detailed body of knowledge that would take a lifetime of study in this one aspect alone. You might like to consider, however, when you come to check the feng shui of your home, that you need to recognise that ch'i flows in different ways throughout buildings as much as it does throughout the human body. Your home, too, will need guarding ch'i and original ch'i.

ORIGINAL CH'I AND YOUR HOME

As ch'i flows it is being constantly attracted to your home – the flow from yin to yang – and ch'i picks up residues from whatever it has passed over or through. Here's the first practical exercise: go and open your front door and look out. What do you see? The original ch'i being drawn into your home will be carrying an echo of whatever it is you can see. Perhaps you're looking out over a beautiful view of countryside, rivers and hills – that's what's being brought into your home. But what if you're looking out at an abattoir? Or a graveyard? A police station? Army barracks? If ch'i has passed through a graveyard immediately before entering your home it will be bringing sorrow and grief with it – and this can be transferred to you. If the ch'i has passed through an abattoir it will be bringing pain and fear – and passing it on to you. Don't panic if your view is somewhat negative. There are various ways of purifying the ch'i as it enters your home and we will look at these later. By the way, this book is not a do-it-for-you-manual. It's more of a teach-you-how-to-do-it-and-then-let-you-do-it-for-yourself. I can't come and look out of your front door for you – you'll have to do that, and then decide what the ch'i will be bringing with it. It won't just be the physical attributes of what it has passed near but also the emotional; the emotional history of a place will be very strong and can affect us in subtle but important ways.

This case study concerns a woman who asked me to look at the feng shui of her house. She was a successful business woman, independent, wealthy and completely confident in her business dealings. It was her relationships that suffered badly. She said that she constantly felt trapped whenever in a relationship; as soon as a new one started she felt claustrophobic and overcome with strong feelings that she had to escape, break free. It may sound a simple solution but one quick look out of her front door indicated a possible source of her feelings. She directly faced a prison and was picking up on all the residue feelings from there. The prison was also to the north of her home which affected the relationship area or enrichment of her life (more about the eight enrichments later) so we had to remedy the ch'i coming from the prison as it entered her home. Once that was done she was able to enter a new relationship successfully and did, in fact, get married within a year. However, she was also aware that her location wasn't ideal and did move to a new home – one that looked out over fields and open countryside.

THE FOUR CARDINAL COMPASS DIRECTIONS

Perhaps we'd better look at the different types of ch'i that flow towards your home. The direction that the ch'i flows from is important. Although the traditional feng shui consultants would have worked with up to 64 compass directions we will limit ourselves to eight – things get exciting enough as it is using only the eight main compass directions. The eight compass directions generate their own ch'i which has its own qualities. But first we need to look at each of the four cardinal compass directions.

- ☺ **South** Symbolised in Chinese culture by the phoenix – known as the Red Bird of the South. The phoenix is called *feng Huang* (it can also be a pheasant, cockerel or any bright bird) and represents luck, the summer, fame and fortune, happiness, light, joy and hope. The ch'i coming from the south is known as *yang ch'i* and it is vigorous ch'i. The south's colour is red. Its element is fire.

- ☺ **North** Symbolised by the tortoise – *Yuan Wu* – the Black Tortoise (can also be a coiled snake, a turtle, and even smoke). The north represents the hidden, the mysterious, winter, sleep, ritual, nurture and caring. The ch'i coming from the North is *ts'ang ch'i* – nurturing ch'i. The north's colour is black. Its element is water.

- ☺ **East** Symbolised by the dragon – *Wen* – the Green Dragon (can also be gold but always a dragon). The east is protective, cultured, wise, spring, kindness and learning. The ch'i coming from the east is *sheng ch'i* – growing ch'i. The east's colour is green. Its element is wood.

- ☺ **West** Symbolised by the tiger – *Wu* – the White Tiger. The west is an area of unpredictability, even danger. It contains warfare and strength, the autumn, anger, suddenness and potential violence. The ch'i coming from the west is *shan ch'i* – changeable ch'i. The west's colour is white. Its element is metal.

These symbolic animals appear throughout Chinese culture, and you now know why – they represent more than just mythical or fabulous beasts, they personify everything about Taoism and feng shui. The compass directions are important, too. If you read the characteristics, for instance, of the west you will realise why China has always been wary of Westerners – it is from the west that sudden violence can strike, it's an area of disruption and unpredictability, not to be trusted. In Hong Kong you will even see buildings with windows that face west painted black to avoid any negative ch'i entering a building.

THE FOUR CHINESE COLOURS

You may have noticed that four colours – red, white, black and gold (or green) – dominate Chinese art, architecture or even fashion; you will see these four colours repeated many times. And, again, you now know why – they represent more than just a colour, they are a compass direction, a quality, an animal, a form of ch'i, a season and even an emotion. When Chinese painters want to say something dramatic they may well use just a flash of one of these colours; to us it may be just that – a colour – but to the Chinese there is a whole lot more going on in that one brush stroke. So feng shui even encompasses an appreciation of Chinese art, or at least an understanding of it. You could visit your local Chinese restaurant and just see how many times these images and colours occur. Imagine how important they are to the whole of Chinese culture.

THE FOUR QUADRANTAL COMPASS POINTS

Once we have an appreciation of the four cardinal, or main, compass directions we can fill in the four quadrantal, or secondary, points – south-east, south-west, north-east and north-west.

You may be wondering why we need this information? It's all to do with the direction your house faces, which is an important part of compass feng shui. Obviously, a house that faces north will receive completely different ch'i, and thus different qualities, from a house which faces south. We will cover all of this in greater depth later – this is just the theory.

- **South-east** This combines the vigorous ch'i of the south with the growing ch'i of the east to produce its own unique creative ch'i.
- **South-west** This direction combines the vigorous south ch'i with the changeable ch'i of the west to produce soothing ch'i.
- **North-east** This combines the nurturing ch'i of the north with the growing ch'i of the east to produce flourishing ch'i.
- **North-west** This combines the nurturing ch'i of the north with the changeable ch'i of the west to produce expansive ch'i.

Below is a list summarising each of the eight compass directions with their relevant key word.

- South – vigorous
- North – nurturing
- East – growing
- West – changing
- South-east – creative
- South-west – soothing
- North-east – flourishing
- North-west – expansive

Whichever direction your house faces, and that is determined by which way your front door faces, will bring a different dominant ch'i with its own unique quality.

Once we know which way our house faces we can begin to determine which ch'i, and which quality, will dominate in our home. You may need a small compass to work out your direction. If you don't have one or prefer not to use one there is a simple way to find out which direction you face at any time. Merely close your eyes and imagine yourself in a room of which you know the compass layout. Suppose your bed is positioned north–south so that when you are in bed your head is in the north and you lie on your right side facing west. No matter where you are, if you imagine yourself in bed in this position you can tell the compass points. If you are facing west it will feel 'right'. If you are facing any other direction it will feel 'wrong' and you will know which way to turn – in your imagination in your bed – to make it feel right. Try this simple technique and see if it works for you. All you have to know is the compass direction of one favourite room or place.

CH'I AND SHA

If you imagine standing in the middle of your house, you can turn in eight different compass directions and you will receive the benefit of the eight different types of ch'i. But what if the ch'i was failing on its way to you and becoming sha? There are eight different types of sha depending on which direction it comes from.

- **South**   Vigorous ch'i degrades to accelerating sha which causes you to feel exhausted.
- **North**   Nurturing ch'i degrades to lingering sha which causes you to feel lethargic.
- **East**   Growing ch'i degrades to overpowering sha which causes you to feel egotistical and vain.

45

- **West** Changeable ch'i degrades to dangerous sha which causes you to act rashly.
- **South-east** Creative ch'i degrades to provoking sha which causes you to feel irritable and headachy.
- **South-west** Soothing ch'i degrades to disruptive sha which causes you to feel angry.
- **North-east** Flourishing ch'i degrades to stagnating sha which causes ill health.
- **North-west** Expansive ch'i degrades to unpredictable sha which causes you to feel unsettled.

If you now look at Figure 3.1 you will see how these eight directions receive their ch'i. You will also notice that there is a definite movement from spring/the east through summer/the south to autumn/the west and finally to winter/the north.

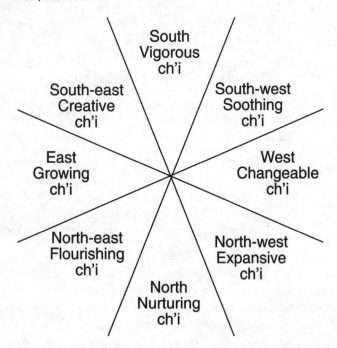

Figure 3.1 Ch'i directions

THE MOVEMENT OF CH'I THROUGH THE YEAR
≡

There is also a logical flow of ch'i. It starts as growing ch'i in the spring (east) becomes vigorous ch'i in the summer (south), becomes changeable ch'i in the autumn (west) and settles to sleepy nurturing ch'i in the winter (north). And the colours also follow a pattern – green in the spring to represent growth; red in the summer for heat; white in the autumn for mists and frosts; and black in the winter for sleep and hibernation.

This also gives us a cycle for the five elements: wood helps fire; fire helps earth (the centre); earth helps metal; metal helps water; and water helps wood. Each of these creates the next in the cycle – but it can also hinder it if the flow is incorrect. You may need to refer back to the element chart in Chapter 2 which may make more sense now that you can see a seasonal flow to feng shui.

THE EIGHT ENRICHMENTS
≡

If you imagine yourself standing in the middle of the world with the eight compass points all around you then you may see yourself as being the centre or hub of a great wheel. If the outer rim of the wheel was joined up into a circle and then each of the eight compass points was also joined up, you'd have an octagon, each segment of which would be ruled by a different ch'i quality (see Figure 3.2).

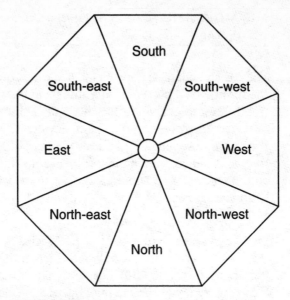

Figure 3.2 The octagon

Now we can put compass directions on these eight segments and write in the ch'i for each one (see Figure 3.3).

Figure 3.3 The eight ch'i areas

Now each ch'i area governs or influences a different area or enrichment of our life. These enrichments take into account just about every facet of life that we need to perform as successful, satisfied adults. You can see that if the ch'i from a particular compass direction has become sha then it will affect that particular area (see Figure 3.4).

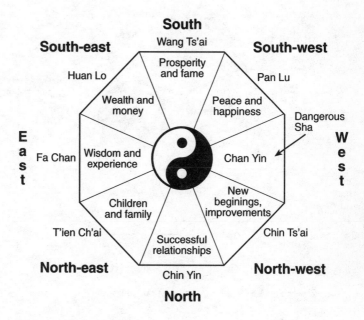

Figure 3.4 The eight enrichments with one sha

This area of sha will need to be remedied if we are to benefit from the properties of ch'i as we should.

THE PAH KWA
≡

The octagon with its eight enrichments is called the Pah Kwa (or bagua as it is sometimes spelt) and it works for an ideal house – that is, one that faces south.

Suppose you have a west-facing house? Or a north-facing house? Then you will need to move the Pah Kwa to find out where your enrichments are (see Figure 3.5).

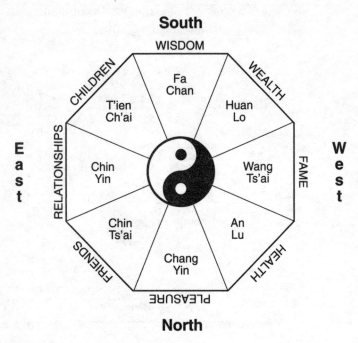

Figure 3.5 Pah Kwa with west-facing house

Later on in this book we will deal with each of the eight directions and how it would affect your house – so don't worry at this stage if you don't live in a south-facing house.

We need now to look at the eight enrichments and see how they affect our lives, and why the differing ch'i affects them. Remember, though, that we are looking at them in an ideal way – as if the house was facing south.

- South – **Wang Ts'ai** – fame, reputation – 1
- South-east – **Huan Lo** – wealth and money – 8

- East – **Fa Chan** – wisdom and experience – 3
- North-east – **T'ien Ch'ai** – children and family – 4
- North – **Chin Yin** – relationships – 9
- North-west – **Chin Ts'ai** – friendships, new beginnings – 2
- West – **Chang Yin** – pleasure and indulgence – 7
- South-west – **An Lu** – health, peace and happiness – 6

Let's see how this looks as a diagram (see Figure 3.6).

South

Figure 3.6 The eight enrichments

The magic square

We will deal with how to overlay the Pah Kwa on your own house in Chapter 4. You will have noticed that each of the enrichments is numbered. If you draw the Pah Kwa out into a square the numbers form a *lo shu*, or magic square. Add the numbers in any direction and they add up to 15.

The lo shu is a very ancient Chinese device used for all sorts of ritualistic magic purposes and its layout is incorporated into many building designs. It is also valuable for 'walking the Nine Palaces', a ritualistic way of checking the feng shui of a building which we will go into in greater depth later.

If you take the lo shu you can also add the Chinese astrological animals, times of day and months of the year (see Figure 3.7). This may give you some indication of where your ideal location or direction might be if you know which Chinese animal you are, or what time of day you feel best at, or even which month suits you best.

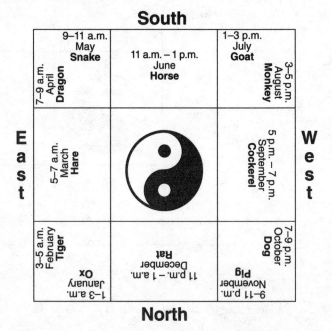

Figure 3.7 Lo shu with astrological animals, times of day and months

The eight enrichments are important to feng shui and we need to look at each in some detail. Remember that we are looking at a house that is facing south.

SOUTH – WANG TS'AI – FAME, REPUTATION

South, Wang Ts'ai, is the most auspicious direction for your front door to face. Wang Ts'ai, fame and reputation, is the area you step out into the world from. This area is where you present your 'face' to the rest of the world. Wang Ts'ai is influenced by what is immediately visible as you open your front door. What do you see? Hopefully a 'good' view – one that is invigorating, hopeful and inspiring – because this is how you will perceive the world. Open your front door on to 'negative' views such as seedy backstreets, factories or rubbish dumps and that will negatively affect your dealings with the outside world. Your emotional horizons are influenced by what is outside your front door – the wider the view the greater your scope for coping with what the world can throw at you. The more limited and narrow the view the more subject to stress and 'loss of face' you will be. The area of Wang Ts'ai is not only what you can see outside your front door but also what you have immediately inside it. What have you got there?

Traditionally, in Western homes, this may well be an area where you keep the equipment you need to step out into the world – your overcoat, umbrella, keys, that sort of thing. It's also the area where the world comes in to you – the place the post arrives bringing bills, letters, junk mail, birthday cards to you. What sort of post do you get? It may be indicative of how the world perceives you – and that is influenced by how you approach the world. Step out from your front door boldly, full of confidence and hope, and that is how the world will greet you. Step out sadly with your head down and that is how the world will accept you – and treat you accordingly.

Ideally, Wang Ts'ai should have elements of the colour red in it. Red is bright and full of life – fire to motivate you in the world. This is the area of the Red Phoenix – the bird of recovery. No matter how bad things have been when you step out from Wang Ts'ai there is always hope of rebirth – a new start. No matter how low you've been brought you can always rebuild, start again.

And what ch'i comes from the south? Vigorous ch'i – ch'i to make you feel fired-up and ready to take on the world – ready to enhance your fame, improve your 'face' and spread your reputation successfully. Vigorous ch'i degrades to accelerating sha. This can cause you to feel exhausted – it all becomes too much for you and you can't go out because the world just seems too much effort to take on. Accelerated sha needs to be remedied to make it vigorous ch'i – we will find out how to do this later on – so you can take on the world again, full of renewed vigour.

SOUTH-EAST – HUAN LO – WEALTH AND MONEY

Huan Lo is the second most important area – according to traditional Chinese feng shui – and this is the second most auspicious place to have your front door. Huan Lo is where you find your magnet to attract money. Look at the area to the left of your front door. What have you got there? This is what is affecting your money-earning potential. Is this a good area? Is it full of light and beauty or dark and ugly and unused? How's your bank balance? Beautiful or dark? Huan Lo benefits from creative ch'i – it creates wealth as it arrives so you may need to check what the ch'i is passing before it arrives in the Huan Lo enrichment. And creative ch'i degrades to provoking sha. This can make you irritable – it can also cause you to spend money too freely on things you don't really need or want. It literally provokes you and you react by trying to buy peace of mind. It's a sort of 'I can't cope so I'll go shopping to cheer myself up' approach to life. We all suffer from it at some time. If it is a serious habit you may well need to remedy this area. If money slips through your fingers faster than water then you need to look closely at this area and see what is causing this. It may sound simplistic but maybe there's a small downstairs cloakroom here with a dripping tap or leaking pipes. I always keep my collection of Chinese 'lucky money' here to attract more and it seems to work. I also keep my account books here that record income. Bills I keep elsewhere as Huan Lo is about attracting money not watching it go out.

SOUTH-WEST – AN LU – HEALTH, PEACE AND HAPPINESS

An Lu is the enrichment to the right of the front door. Ideally, it will face south-west, ready to benefit from the soothing ch'i that flows from this direction. Soothing ch'i helps your health by easing stress. It also enables you to find peace and happiness here. This should be an area where you can relax and take time out; an area just for you, dedicated to your own needs during quiet times. What have you got here? How do you think it might affect your health? Soothing ch'i degrades to disruptive sha. This can cause you to feel angry – and anger is a symptom of stress. And how can you relax and enjoy peace and happiness if you're always feeling angry? Check this area carefully and make sure it is comfortable and relaxing, ready to benefit from the soothing ch'i.

EAST – FA CHAN – WISDOM AND EXPERIENCE

In Chinese culture the Dragon is a symbol of wisdom and benevolence and the Dragon lives in the east. What better place to have Fa Chan, wisdom and experience, where it can benefit from all that Dragon energy? Ideally, here you'd have well-rounded green hills – the back of the sleeping Dragon – and in the enrichment you'd provide a place to study and keep your scholastic honours. What do you have in your Fa Chan? In the West we tend to think that education ceases when we leave school, whereas the Taoists see it as an ongoing process – the longer we live the more we need to know, and the longer we have to learn. For the Chinese, growing into wisdom is as important as being rich is in the West. Being wise lasts longer, is less subject to a recession, benefits those around us more and helps us find satisfaction in our lives more fully. Without wisdom and experience we cannot mature and grow – and pass on that wisdom to our children and help them take their place in the world.

Fa Chan benefits from growing ch'i – and we grow in wisdom and experience every day. The Dragon is the symbol of spring – each day has the potential to teach us more than we knew yesterday, to grow in stature and maturity. Growing ch'i degrades to overpowering sha which causes us to feel egotistic and vain – we feel we 'know it all' and try to tell everyone around us how wise we are. It might be better to remedy this sha and, as the Tao says, 'those that know keep silent'.

WEST – CHANG YIN – PLEASURE AND INDULGENCE

Chang Yin is the enrichment governed by the White Tiger – unpredictable and potentially dangerous. Ideally, to the west of your home you'd have a small lake surrounded by wildflowers to calm the enormous power of the Tiger. Too big a lake and the Tiger will devour you; too small and there will be no excitement in your life. Chang Yin is the enrichment where you'd entertain if that's how you seek your pleasure. It's an ideal place to have your dining room where you can serve delicious meals to your friends and indulge yourself. We all need to be indulged from time to time and Chang Yin is the place to do it. It benefits from changeable ch'i – we wouldn't want all pleasure, all indulgence, but we do need it occasionally. Changeable ch'i is unpredictable – like the power of the Tiger – and can turn to dangerous sha easily which can cause us to act rashly – perhaps drink a little too much or take things too easily and become lazy. The blowing wind of changeable ch'i refreshes us and keeps us on our toes but too much and we can feel unsettled and this is what causes the rashness. This is not a place to make decisions or to negotiate contracts but rather a place to unwind and enjoy ourselves.

NORTH – CHIN YIN – RELATIONSHIPS

Traditionally, Chin Yin is the enrichment that relates to marriage. However, here in the West there is a tendency towards 'relationships' rather than marriage so that's how I refer to it. Chin Yin is situated in the north, ideally, as this is the area we wish to nurture. The Chinese believe that a successful marriage is very important. How can you find satisfaction in this world without your soul mate, your ideal partner? And once we have found such a person we have to look after the relationship to make it work. We have to protect it and care for it or it will fail. Relationships benefit from the nurturing ch'i of the north but if it is allowed to degrade to lingering sha it causes lethargy – and that is the biggest cause of failure in any relationship. If we don't work at it and endeavour to keep it fresh and exciting it will atrophy and die. It makes sense to keep the area of relationships at the back of the house, in the north, to protect our loved ones and keep them safe. This is why T'ien Ch'ai, children and family, is also here. Ideally, we'd have the black hills of the tortoise behind us to protect the most vulnerable members of our family. Chin Yin is traditionally associated with an area of warmth and sleepiness. Here we can have the family fireside and enjoy the nurturing ch'i.

NORTH EAST – T'IEN CH'AI – CHILDREN AND FAMILY

T'ien Ch'ai is the family enrichment. Personally this is the area in which I like to feed young babies and keep a comfortable chair by the fire to read stories to children, even keep the television there if that's what it takes to keep them entertained. T'ien Ch'ai benefits from flourishing ch'i, and what could be better for growing children? However, it degrades to stagnating sha which is a cause of ill health.

Check this area carefully if you want your children to flourish and not suffer from endless colds and the sort of minor irritations that affect infants. T'ien Ch'ai enjoys both the nurturing power of the Black Tortoise and the wisdom of the Green Dragon, and that is probably all that children really need – your experience and your love – for them to flourish and grow healthily and well. T'ien Ch'ai is probably the most protected enrichment and that is where children need to be, safe and secure nestling between the sleepy hills of the north and the wise hills of the east.

*N*ORTH-WEST – CHIN TS'AI – FRIENDSHIPS, NEW BEGINNINGS

Chin Ts'ai is the ideal enrichment for sounding out new ideas, new projects. Here we can discuss our plans for the future, prepare for our holidays, chat to friends and get their advice. This is an enrichment where improvements in our life will begin. It benefits from expansive ch'i combining the nurture of the north with the change blowing in from the west. A good place to dream a little, to wish a little, to allow your imagination to take wing and chance all those plans you'd never dared hope for. I always like to keep a note pad and pen in this area as I always seem to be getting new ideas here. I write them down before I forget them. My friends tend to gravitate naturally towards this area when they visit; that could be something to do with the fact that this is where I keep the gin and tonics, or it might just be that they, too, like to enjoy that expansive ch'i. I have to limit them a little or we find we've sat up half the night talking new plans and ideas. Watch the expansive ch'i, though, as it degrades to unpredictable sha. If left unchecked or unremedied it can cause friends to suddenly stop dropping in, or your plans to come to nothing – or to be altered into something you didn't want. Unpredictable sha causes you to feel unsettled and restless. You begin to feel overwhelmed – what's the use of planning anything if nothing ever happens?

The enrichments of your desk

The eight enrichments apply to your whole house – on each floor. But they can also apply to an individual room or even a small area such as a desk which can be divided into the eight enrichments and each area allocated a specific purpose or focus. For instance, you might like to keep a photograph of your children in the top right-hand corner of your desk for your t'ien ch'ai enrichment – or how about your computer and screen: all those files are your children as well. You can keep a photo of your loved one directly in front of you at the back of the desk where you can gaze on him or her lovingly as you work; I also keep a lamp here to illuminate my relationship and make it brighter. I keep my dictionaries and reference books on the right-hand edge – fa chan, wisdom and experience; a coffee pot on the left-hand edge – chan yin, pleasure and indulgence. In the bottom-right corner I keep my computer mouse – constantly clicking up new money. In the top left-hand corner I keep a note pad to jot down new ideas and suggestions for future projects. The bit where I sit is my wang ts'ai, my fame. This is where I work, my passport to the world – and my reputation, of course. And on the bottom-left corner of my desk I keep a small cassette player to soothe me with restful music while I am working.

This is how the eight enrichments can apply to even a quite small area. Now I expect you want to know how to remedy areas that don't function as well as they might, or remedy areas where you might be encountering problems.

THE EIGHT REMEDIES

It seems logical that if there are eight compass directions, eight types of ch'i, eight types of sha and eight enrichments, then there should be eight remedies – and there are, of course.

For ch'i to bring you health and good fortune it must be allowed to flow in its natural way – this is in smooth curves and at the proper speed. Too fast and it will cause disruption and allow anger to manifest. Too slow and it will stagnate and cause lethargy and depression. Ch'i likes to flow gently through open spaces and if you provide clutter and untidy areas it will become confused and unfocused. Ch'i likes harmony and beauty, cleanliness and balance. You should be aware of what the ch'i has flowed through or near before it arrives at your home, as it is liable to pick up residues of any unpleasant occurrences. Ch'i dislikes straight lines that cause it to pick up speed and flow too quickly. It also dislikes being trapped in small confined areas. When you walk the Nine Palaces, which we will deal with later on, you can imagine yourself being the ch'i and you can ask yourself if you, too, could flow smoothly through your home or would you be obstructed, confused, confined, accelerated or stagnated? If you find that the ch'i is not being allowed to flow as freely as it needs to then you may well find it manifests in your life as lack of money, an unfortunate relationship, an inability to relax, loss of friends, noisy and badly behaved children or even perhaps ill health. If the ch'i is being impeded in any way you will need one of the eight remedies which are:

- light
- sound
- colour
- life
- movement
- stillness
- mechanical objects
- straight lines

*L*IGHT

This includes lights, mirrors and reflective surfaces. Mirrors are probably the mostly widely known feng shui remedy. They can be used in most situations. They will reflect bad ch'i, sha, back out of a building, encourage good ch'i in by capturing a pleasant view from outside, lighten and enlarge small, dark rooms, deflect ch'i around hidden corners, even alter and change the psychology of a room. Used in conjunction with lamps they can transform a room completely. Lights should be as bright as possible without causing glare. You should never be able to see a bare bulb. The Chinese use a lot of lights outside the house and in the garden to fill in missing or dead ch'i. It's not something we tend to make use of in the West but lights can enhance a dull garden, especially at night.

Traditionally, in China, special octagonal mirrors have always been used to deflect unpleasant ch'i back to where it has come from. The mirrors would be placed facing outwards towards whatever it was that was regarded as incorrect. You can use any small mirror to do the same. If your house faces a graveyard or factory then a small mirror placed to reflect the sha will improve the ch'i entering your home. Any dark areas or corners of your home can be livened up by placing good quality lamps in them. Soft lighting is best to create harmony. You can also use mirrors to encourage light into darker areas, or place them at the end of long corridors to slow the ch'i down.

Sound

Most people associate Chinese culture with wind chimes without realising that they are an important feng shui remedy. Anything that makes sound can also be used: bells, metal mobiles, bamboo tubes, etc. Melodic noises can help break up stagnant ch'i by causing swirls and eddies of sound in the air. Wind chimes also act as gentle alarms to tell us when someone has entered our house. Pleasing and harmonious sounds are also good attractants of lucky ch'i: they are said to encourage wealth into buildings. The sound of water flowing is very beneficial. Fountains can be seen both as movement and sound.

Harsh noises cause ch'i to become jangled and inharmonious. You can use wind chimes, bells, even the sound of water fountains to create a harmony of sound and soothe the ch'i. Sound is traditionally associated with your friends enrichment so you can play your CD player here and provide your guests with harmonious music.

COLOUR

The Chinese are great believers in using colour to stimulate the flow of ch'i, especially the four dominant colours of red, white, gold/green and black which we looked at earlier. These are lucky colours associated with attracting fame, activity, wisdom and wealth. In the West we usually prefer more subtle colour schemes but it is useful to remember that a sudden patch of bright, strong colour in a stagnating room can stimulate ch'i quite effectively.

Any area where you feel stressed or irritable should be decorated simply in pale colours, white is best, and then a single, simple flash of bright colour introduced to focus the ch'i and keep it vibrant. Colour is traditionally associated with your children enrichment, which is probably why all those children's toys are such bright colours.

LIFE

Plants are mainly used to fill in blank areas where there isn't any ch'i or to help ch'i that is stagnating to 'come to life' again. They can be used to hide disruptive sharp corners that poke into rooms and stimulate ch'i in areas where it might linger. Large plants can be used to slow ch'i down when it is being directed too quickly along straight lines. Fish in aquariums are also used for the same purpose. The Chinese for 'fish' and for 'money' is the same word so they often use fish to represent wealth. That's why you will often see fish tanks next to the cash register in Chinese restaurants – it encourages you to spend freely.

When ch'i is weakening or causing a depletion of energy or life force you need to introduce some element of life into an area. Pot plants are best but they should have rounded leaves. Cut flowers aren't a good idea as their ch'i is leaking away as they die, and dried flowers are frowned on as they have no life left in them. Plants should not be left untended or allowed to get dusty, and traditionally they have been associated with your money enrichment. The Chinese use fish in tanks to introduce life into an area. If you want to do the same you should use an odd number of fish, and goldfish are recommended.

MOVEMENT

Wherever ch'i needs to be stimulated or deflected use a moving object. The Chinese use flags, silk banners, ribbons, fountains, wind chimes, mobiles and weather vanes. Moving objects should use the natural power of the wind if possible and be made of natural materials.

The smoke from incense can be regarded as movement and be used beneficially but obviously only short term.

Flowing water brings ch'i to the building but it should move gently and gurgle rather than roar. An ideal location for a house is one where it faces south with a babbling brook in the south-east bringing in lots of money.

Movement is associated with your relationship enrichment, and this is where we always need movement to stop things getting stale and being taken for granted.

STILLNESS

Any large, inanimate object such as a statue or large rock can bring a stillness to an otherwise too-fast ch'i area. This is especially beneficial in gardens where the path to a front gate can cause the ch'i to leave too quickly. Any statues used should blend harmoniously into your home and have a particular significance for you. You can use large natural objects like driftwood or a bleached gnarled branch.

Traditionally, in China there would be an area in the home where a statue would be placed to provide a focus for spirituality. This would often be a Buddha but you could use any large, beautiful object from a piece of driftwood to an unusual stone. It should be simple but exquisite, and it will slow ch'i down and help purify it. Traditionally associated with your pleasure enrichment, a still object will allow you many happy hours' relaxing and contemplating natural beauty or the perfection of a craftsperson's labour.

MECHANICAL OBJECTS

In traditional feng shui this usually meant machinery or tools but nowadays it can be extended to include any electrical equipment we need to use: televisions, stereos, electrical fans, and probably most important of all – computers. Electricity and ch'i need to be harmoniously regarded if they are not to clash: both need to be treated with respect. Electrical equipment can stimulate ch'i but sometimes it can overdo it, so keep it to the minimum.

Anything mechanical or manufactured that does a job of work, or is a tool, can be used to stir up dull ch'i – anything from a television to an electric kettle. You need to be careful as mechanical devices tend to be very strong remedies. Traditionally, they have been associated with your education enrichment, so this is a perfect place to keep your computer.

STRAIGHT LINES

The Chinese use flutes, swords, scrolls, bamboo tubes and fans to break up ch'i when it moves heavily or sluggishly, especially along beams and down long corridors. The straight lines are hung at an angle to create the Pah Kwa octagonal shape and that helps to direct the ch'i away from the beam or corridor and back into the rooms.

Although we have talked of ch'i disliking straight lines, there are times when ch'i needs to be enlivened or interrupted.

Perhaps you have beams that ch'i can flow along too quickly; you can use anything that has straight lines such as the items described above – even swords – to break the ch'i up and deflect it into the room. Straight lines have traditionally been associated with your health enrichment.

Using remedies

Perhaps you need some tips on how to recognise when you need a remedy? Check each of the eight areas of your life. How are your finances? Your relationship? Your health? Your fame and reputation? Check each one in turn. If you are happy with that particular area of your life then the chances are that you don't need a remedy there. But if you are experiencing problems you may well need to do some work on that area. Let's suppose it's your finances that are suffering a bit. You check the area and find that your money enrichment happens to fall in your dining room. Perhaps you've been eating all your money? If you visit a Chinese restaurant you may well see, as we said earlier, a fish tank near the cash register – this is to encourage money to come to life. Perhaps you could try a fish tank in your dining room? Or a large plant to encourage the ch'i to provide good fortunes?

Suppose it's your relationship that is suffering and you check that enrichment area and find it falls in your study. Perhaps you have been devoting too much time to work? Or are you and your partner in business together and you don't spend enough time together away from work? You could try introducing a wind chime above your desk to stir the ch'i up, or how about one of those executive desk toys that moves? Or if you have your computer here you could try running a moving 'screen saver' when you're not using it.

The thing to remember with remedies is that you can't do any harm by introducing one into an area. If it's the wrong one you will simply remain static – there'll be no improvement. Sometimes you have to experiment and move things around before you produce a positive result.

What ch'i likes

Remember that ch'i likes harmony, gentle curves, beauty, spaciousness, and order. It dislikes disorder, clutter, straight lines and neglected areas. Sometimes you have to completely revamp your house – not because the decoration is wrong but because decay and neglect have set in. Ch'i likes spring cleaning and freshness. Sometimes that's all you need to do to an area to benefit from better ch'i – tidy up and spring clean. Our homes should reflect the inner self. If we are cluttered and confused inside, our home will reflect that. By clearing out the debris externally we can shift the inner clutter and revitalise ourselves. By focusing on a particular enrichment of our life we have already taken a major step towards improvement.

The eight remedies and their ideal enrichments

Each of these eight remedies has a particular enrichment area that it works best in:

- **Light** – associated with your **fame** enrichment
- **Sound** – associated with your **friends** enrichment
- **Colour** – associated with your **children** enrichment
- **Life** – associated with your **money** enrichment
- **Movement** – associated with your **relationship** enrichment
- **Stillness** – associated with your **pleasure** enrichment
- **Mechanical objects** – associated with your **education** enrichment
- **Straight lines** – associated with your **health** enrichment

However, this works properly only with a south-facing home. If your house faces another direction we will deal with that in Chapter 4.

THE BASIC PRINCIPLES OF FENG SHUI

In Chapters 2 and 3 we have covered the basic principles upon which feng shui is based. It's a lot of information to take in at once so you might be better off remembering it in easy stages.

To recap: There are eight directions, eight types of ch'i, eight types of sha, eight remedies and eight enrichments. These all fit together rather like a jigsaw puzzle. If one of them is 'wrong' or out of place it can throw everything else out. By correcting the faulty piece the rest falls into place and life becomes smooth and successful again. Identifying the fault is dealt with in Chapter 4 – practical feng shui.

4

HOUSE DIRECTIONS

It's a warm wind, the west wind, full of birds' cries;
I never hear the west wind but tears are in my eyes.
For it comes from the west lands, the old brown hills,
And April's in the west wind, and daffodils.

JOHN MASEFIELD

WHICH WAY DOES YOUR HOUSE FACE?

In this chapter we will look at the eight different directions your house can face. Remember the direction is set by the direction of your front door. You may use a side entrance, climb in through a window, abseil down from the roof – and it won't make a blind bit of difference. The house direction is set by the front door direction: open your front door and face west and you have a west-facing house; open your front door to the north-east and you have a north-east facing house. If you choose to use another entrance then that says something pretty significant about you and your dwelling – and one you should look carefully at. Perhaps if you use a different entrance – such as a side entrance – you may be seeking a different enrichment as the dominant one, or a different ch'i to work with, or even a different element type to live with. We will explore this more later.

YIN/YANG DIRECTIONS
≡

Before we look at the different house directions, there is an interesting part of feng shui about yin and yang that you may have already noticed from the previous chapters, but it needs emphasising. There are four yang directions and four yin directions.

The four yang directions

- ☻ East – li – ☰☰
- ☻ South-east – tui – ☱☱
- ☻ South – ch'ien – ☰
- ☻ South-west – h'sun – ☴☴

These four directions correspond, in the ideal, favoured south-facing house, to four enrichments:

- ☻ Fa Chan – wisdom and experience
- ☻ Huan Lo – wealth and possessions
- ☻ Wang Ts'ai – fame and reputation
- ☻ An Lu – health and peace

These are known as the four personal enrichments. These are all yang, all corresponding with the 'male' principle. The 'I' part of life. They are concerned with the individual: an individual's own personal wisdom, wealth, fame and health.

The four yin directions

- ☻ West – kan – ☵☵
- ☻ North-west – ken – ☶☶
- ☻ North – kun – ☷☷
- ☻ North-east – chen – ☳☳

These four yin directions correspond, in an ideal south-facing house, to four yin enrichments:

- Chang Yin – pleasure and indulgence
- Chin Ts'ai – friends and new beginnings
- Chin Yin – relationships and marriage
- T'ien Ch'ai – children and family

These are the four yin enrichments. They correspond with the yin or 'female' principle. They are all to do with 'us'. They are known as the four collective enrichments.

Yin and yang aspects of the home

You may have noticed the four yang personal enrichments are all located at the front of the house whereas the four yin collective enrichments are located at the back of the house.

- The front of a house is yang – personal, confident, bold, outward.
- The back of a house is yin – collective, nurturing, protective, inward.

It's an interesting part of house design that if you want to know the true history of a house always look first at the back. The front gets changed a lot. New frontages are added and fashions change. The front is a visible sign of an occupant's personality. The back, however, undergoes less change. The front may be radically altered but the back will remain pretty much the same as when the house was first built. The back is less visible so is less subject to fashion, but it is more representative of the inner personality of a house.

The front, yang aspect of a house is where we park the car – a visible sign of us being out in the world. The back is where we relax in private, where we play with our children. A visitor coming to the front door rings a bell and waits for us to answer. But what if the same visitor walks unannounced round the back and straight into the back garden or in through the door? How do we feel? Is it not quite a shock to our system? An intrusion on our privacy? The visitor has invaded our yin and disturbed us. The same visitor coming to the front door is respecting the yang and is welcomed.

I'm sure you can think of other examples of this. But by now you may be saying that your house doesn't face south and therefore can't be ideal. The word 'ideal' isn't ideal. The early feng shui practitioners recommended that a house should face south and based all their calculations on that. It is a most beneficial direction, and if they were consulted before a house was built would always recommended it. You probably bought or rented your home long after it was built, and therefore inherited its direction without thinking about it. Perhaps subconsciously you selected a different direction because each of the eight directions does actually suit different people. I personally don't thrive in a south-facing house and always go for one that faces north or north-east but that's to do with the make-up of my personality.

WALKING THE NINE PALACES

In ancient China when a house was first built no one would live in it until the local Taoist priest had been along and blessed it. The priest would have probably been instrumental in helping with the design of the house anyway. The priest would 'walk the Nine Palaces'. This entails walking through the house according to a ritual which is based on the lo shu – the magic square (see Chapter 3). You should always use this ritualistic way of walking through your home whenever you need to check any of the enrichments. Walking the Nine Palaces mentally fixes what you are actually doing. This isn't a casual stroll through your home wondering if you need to redecorate. You are following an ancient way and those who have gone before you would appreciate your time and respect in continuing the tradition.

Taking your time

In the West we tend to rush at things too much. This is an Eastern philosophy and one that goes on at a slower pace. Take your time and enjoy the journey. If you rush through walking the Nine Palaces you may miss that tiny detail that will change things for you. It's very easy to think we 'know it all', that all we have to do is have a quick check and everything will be fine. If you rush this you don't allow your home the space to speak to you, to tell you what it feels is wrong and what it would like corrected. Feng shui is not an exact science, it can't be proved by reason or logic. It functions on a different level from anything else we've ever encountered and we need to open channels into our intuitive nature. The Taoist priests knew this, and when they walked the Nine Palaces with the house's new owner they would take their time, stopping in each enrichment to allow the owner and the house to get acquainted, to become one with each other. In each enrichment they would have lit some incense and burnt paper prayers – these were written in traditional Chinese calligraphy on rice paper: they flare up quickly and the burnt embers rise upwards taking the prayer heavenwards.

Your home as a living entity

In the West we may feel that a home is just somewhere to rest up for a bit before going back to work. But in China a home is seen as a living entity. It needs breath and life for it to enrich us and protect us properly. If we neglect our relationship with our home then we will be that much poorer in spirit for it. Feng shui is about relearning this. The fabric of the building is as important as the decor; the decor as important as the furnishings; the furnishings as important as the light, air and breath of the house. And all of these are equally as important as us, the living occupants of the house. Recently in the West some research has been done on the effects of living under or near overhead power lines and electricity pylons. Evidence does seem to point to living in such locations as being injurious to health. Feng shui would have told you that without any research being done, papers compiled, scientists involved, doctors consulted or anyone having to be at risk. If we all lived according to stricter feng shui principles and respected the landscape and environment, the pylons would never have been erected in the first place and no one need have suffered.

The nine questions

Back to the Nine Palaces. You start at your front door which we will call enrichment **1**. At each enrichment stop and listen. As you are walking the Nine Palaces you need to ask nine questions in each enrichment.

- ☻ How does this area feel to you?
- ☻ How do you feel about it?
- ☻ What would you change in this enrichment?
- ☻ What feels right here?
- ☻ What feels wrong?
- ☻ What problems have you encountered in your life that relate to this enrichment?
- ☻ What can you take away from this area?
- ☻ What is missing from this area?
- ☻ If you were starting from scratch would you have this area the same as it is now?

Your front door is **1** – Wang Ts'ai – your fame area. Open your front door, look out and ask the nine questions. When, and only when, you are satisfied with the answers should you move on to the next area. Imagine you have that Taoist priest standing with you and that he is asking the questions. What answers would you give him? Perhaps you might like to do this exercise with someone you really trust, someone whose advice and guidance you respect. Get that person to ask you the nine questions. You may answer differently if you have to speak out loud. It's as if having to justify the answers to another person has the capacity to make us really sure of what we feel and say about a particular area.

Once you have finished with your assessment of 1 – Wang Ts'ai – then you can move on to **2** – Chin Ts'ai – friends and new beginnings. This area you will find is immediately to the right at the back of your home – the back, right-hand corner – assuming, as we will for all these directions, that you are facing the front door. Once you have asked everything here you can move on. Sometimes this walking the Nine Palaces can take quite a while. You should allow at least a whole day for this – you get side tracked, caught up in examining the minutest detail of not only how and where you live but also why and what for. The nine questions may spark off all sorts of unexpected lines of inquiry – so take your time, this is nothing to be rushed.

Move on to **3** – Fa Chan – your wisdom and experience enrichment. This you will find along the left-hand side of your home. Again ask the questions and when you are ready, move on to **4** – T'ien Ch'ai – children and family. This you will find immediately behind 3 – Fa Chan. These two enrichments are connected, they flow into each other. Remember that your 'children' may not be your physical offspring, although T'ien Ch'ai is usually taken to mean just that. In this area you should again ask the nine questions and be satisfied with the answers before you move on to 5 the very centre of your home.

5 – Jen Hsin – the centre is not an enrichment but it is known as *Jen Hsin* – which can only really be translated as 'love of the heart'. This is the very centre of your home, the heart, and it deserves special consideration. If you are not sure exactly where the centre of your home lies then perhaps it may be worth measuring it. You can pace out two diagonal lines between the four corners of your home and then where they intersect will be Jen Hsin. Once you've found it you only have to see what you've got there to see what your home revolves around. This is the pivot, the very centre and your home, and possibly your life, revolves around this heart centre. If you are unhappy about what you have here, or you feel that this is not the right thing for your home to rotate around, then change it. Replace whatever you have here with something more suitable. This is quite a surprising exercise to do and you may be in for a shock when you discover what it is that forms the heart centre of your home.

I visited one home where I carried out this exercise to find Jen Hsin. The owner felt that her life was dark and depressing and she wanted to change things. She had carried out considerable redecoration and worked according to correct feng shui principles. She had cleared out a lot of clutter and freed up a lot of space. The lines of her home were clean and curvaceous and obviously attracted a lot of positive and responsive ch'i, but things still weren't quite right.

At Jen Hsin we found a possible source of her problems. The very centre of her home was actually in a dark understairs cupboard – and this was where she had moved all the clutter to. Once we had cleared it all out the owner realised she could cut away the surrounding woodwork and open the whole area up. She did so and moved a small desk into the area with a reading lamp. She painted the walls white and filled it with plants. Within a short time she was reporting that her life was on a positive up again. She had been offered a lucrative job, met a new man, was getting on better with her two grown-up sons and felt fitter and better than she had in a long time. Even her social life was improving. It may all be coincidence but things only changed once she had paid a little time and attention to Jen Hsin.

Once you have finished at 5 you move on to **6** – An Lu –
your health, peace and happiness enrichment. This area you
will find to the right of the front of your home – the right-
hand corner, if you like. Again, ask the nine questions and,
when you are ready, you can move on to **7** – Chang Yin –
pleasure and indulgence. This area is the right-hand side of
your home directly behind your An Lu. While you are
checking out your pleasure and indulgence enrichment you
can sit down, and see if this area really is as comfortable as
it ought to be.

Once you have finished being comfortable you can move
on to **8** – Huan Lo – wealth and possessions. This is the left-
hand corner of your home. Again, ask the nine questions
and when you are ready move on to **9** – Chin Yin –
relationships. This is the very back of your home nestling
between T'ien Ch'ai, children and family, and Chin Ts'ai,
friends. Perhaps here you should be asking the questions
with your partner.

Once you have finished with Chin Yin, you should go back
to **1** – Wang Ts'ai, fame and reputation. Here you should
again check everything is in order. During this walking of
the Nine Palaces you may have changed many things and
you need to just check that the first area is still in harmony,
in balance, with all the changes you have made.

From yang to yin, from yin to yang

You may have noticed that as you walk the Nine Palaces
you are constantly crossing from a yang area to a yin area,
and back to a yang area. As you move between yin and
yang, yang and yin, see how the mood of each area
changes. Yin areas should be as light and bright as possible;
yang areas can be darker and quieter. The principle of yin
and yang is that they always seek the opposite – so you can
provide it by knowing which each wants to be in harmony.

The eight-pointed star

You may also have noticed the shape of the ground plan you are tracing as you walk. This strange, eight-pointed star shape is designed so that you cross and re-cross each area the same number of times, and so that you always move between yin and yang. The order you are walking in terms of enrichments is: fame to friends to wisdom to children to health to pleasure to wealth to relationships, and back to fame. And the order you walk the Nine Palaces in terms of compass directions is: south to north-west to east to north-east to south-west to west to south-east to north, and back to south for a south-facing home. Obviously if your home faces a direction other than south, this compass order will be different.

Let's look at the eight directions in which your house could face. Remember that your front door opens on to the compass direction.

THE FOUR YANG DIRECTION HOUSES

SOUTH-FACING HOUSE – THE PUBLIC PERSON'S HOME

This is the home of the politician, the diplomat, the entertainer, the celebrity, the showbusiness mogul, the writer, the fashion designer, the film star, the movers and shakers. Which are you? This is a very yang home – vigorous, creative – out in the world full of energy and light.

WANG TS'AI – SOUTH FACING – FAME AND REPUTATION

Your fame benefits from vigorous ch'i but can suffer from accelerating sha. How can we express this? Perhaps your fame is vigorous but you could be propelled into the limelight too quickly – avoid the media if you think your

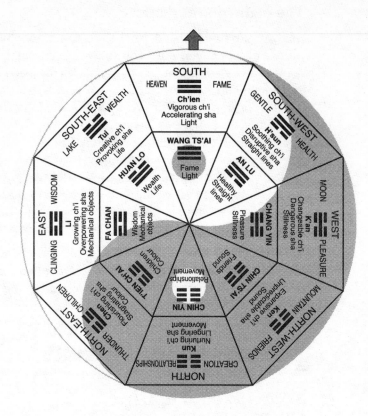

Figure 4.1 The south-facing house

ch'i has become sha. This is an area that benefits from lots of light – this shines on your fame like a spot light – or the flash of a camera.

HUAN LO – SOUTH-EAST FACING – WEALTH AND POSSESSIONS

Your wealth benefits from creative ch'i but can deteriorate into provoking sha. As you have a south-facing house you probably work in the public eye, perhaps in some creative field – a writer, an artist, or most probably a communicator of some sort? When you are working in the ideal field for you by using your creative talents you can be successful when it comes to earning money – but beware the provoking sha. This can cause you to walk out on obligations or climb on a high horse once too often. You are concerned with your image and shouldn't want to engage in any activities that could jeopardise that public face. Fill this area with life – your plants here should be as big, as bold, as bright as you'd like your earnings to be.

FA CHAN – EAST FACING – WISDOM AND EXPERIENCE

This is enjoying growing ch'i and should continue to do so unless it degrades to overpowering sha. Are you trying to run before you can walk? Caution is needed in developing your talents. You shouldn't take on anything more than you know you can cope with – or know you are qualified to do. With your need to be in the public eye it's all too easy to say 'yes' to projects that aren't really suitable for you, not just yet anyway. This area needs a serious mechanical object to enhance all that wisdom and help you gain experience.

T'IEN CH'AI – NORTH-EAST FACING – CHILDREN AND FAMILY

Here, if you let it, you can enjoy flourishing ch'i. A good place for you to be but how sure are you that you can cope with the noise? This is the area of the thunder; it's arousing and colourful but if neglected the ch'i becomes stagnating sha. There is a time to enjoy having a family – and a time to be at peace with them. With your wisdom enrichment in the east it indicates that maybe you are not quite ready yet – you've too much to do out in the world. This area needs colour to be activated – big, bright swathes of primary colours.

CHIN YIN – NORTH FACING – RELATIONSHIPS AND MARRIAGE

This is where your relationships are supposed to be – quiet and sustaining, in the north area of your home and life. The ch'i here is nurturing and you can be enveloped in warmth, love and comfort. If you neglect this area the ch'i becomes lingering sha which can make you question everything too much – and dwell on past mistakes too much – and past hurts. Fill this area with movement.

CHIN TS'AI – NORTH-WEST FACING – FRIENDS AND NEW BEGINNINGS

This is an area enjoying expansive ch'i. Maybe as your fame spreads people are attracted to you in droves. But the ch'i can become unpredictable sha. You need to incorporate the stillness of the mountain that symbolises the north-west into this area. You also need to fill this area with sound to harmonise the sha. Does that give you any ideas? How about flute music playing on your hi-fi? Or pan pipes? The sound here should be clear with the bright stillness of the early morning light on a mountain top.

CHANG YIN – WEST FACING – PLEASURE AND INDULGENCE

When the press have all gone home and your friends have given you some peace and quiet then this is the area to come to, to be alone, to relax and recuperate. The ch'i here is changeable and needs to be calmed and balanced with a stillness remedy. Here you could keep that one perfect piece of statuary that you could sit and admire for hours; something to motivate you; something to bring you inspiration and beauty. If you don't learn to relax and enjoy this space the ch'i has the potential to degenerate into dangerous sha – this can cause stress problems and make you irritable and prone to what the Chinese call 'acts of madness' – these are moments of rashness caused by the sha from the west at its full intensity which it has the potential to reach when you live in a south-facing home.

AN LU – SOUTH-WEST FACING – HEALTH AND PEACE

The ch'i here is soothing and needs to be encouraged with straight lines. This area is gentle like a soft breeze and can bring you great peace and good health – but it is a delicate ch'i and can become disruptive sha easily. It needs to be channelled and guided. Keep this area clear and spacious to allow that tender soothing ch'i a chance to expand and bring you the health, vigour and stamina you need to enjoy this public figure's home.

SOUTH-EAST-FACING HOUSE – THE BUSINESS PERSON'S HOME

This is the home of the entrepreneur, the businessperson, the broker, the financier, the tycoon, the money mogul, the traders, the shopkeeper, the 'I know how I can make money out of that' sort of person.

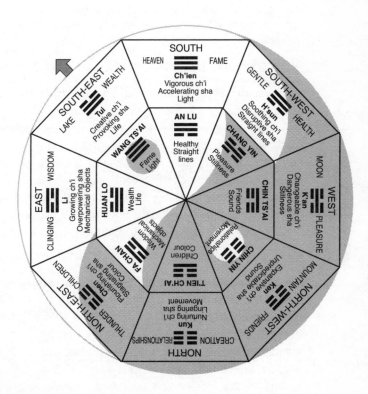

Figure 4.2 The south-east-facing house

WANG TS'AI – SOUTH-EAST FACING – FAME AND REPUTATION

Here you step out of your front door straight into the wealth and possessions area of life. This is your area. Here you are happy. What could be better than enjoying all that creative ch'i and using it to make yourself richer and your family better off. There is no loss of face in enjoying the comforts that wealth can bring. This is the second most-favoured house direction, according to traditional feng shui teachings. However, creative ch'i can become provoking sha. How does it provoke you? Are you driven to accumulate more and more? Does the effort of keeping it become harder? You should settle this area, if it has become problematic in any way, by using a combination of life and light. What does that suggest to you? Perhaps a well-lit aquarium?

HUAN LO – EAST FACING – WEALTH AND POSSESSIONS

Your wealth will come from what you already know – this is a wealth enrichment in the east which is your experience. The ch'i here is growing – how can you fail to make money if you work with what you already know or have. Follow your intuition. The ch'i here can become overpowering – fill this area with life and mechanical tools. How will you do that? You could use plants and make them functional – herbs perhaps? This would be ideal if your kitchen happens to fall in this area. Or how about an automatic cat-feeder here?

FA CHAN – NORTH-EAST FACING – WISDOM AND EXPERIENCE

Here you have a yang enrichment benefiting from yin flourishing ch'i. This is a good combination as it makes your experience well balanced – it gives you a world perspective that others may lack. However, the ch'i can become stagnating sha which can stop any further growth in your wisdom enrichment. You need to combine both colour and a mechanical object in this area. And how about a brightly coloured set of encyclopaedias? This would stimulate the ch'i as well as increasing your learning.

T'IEN CH'AI – NORTH FACING – CHILDREN AND FAMILY

A good yin enrichment in almost its ideal location. Here the ch'i is nurturing which makes you protective towards your family. However, the ch'i can become lingering sha which could make you overprotective. To counteract this you should incorporate both movement and colour – one of those spinning crystals hung in the window perhaps? Or how about a colourful screen-saver if you keep your computer in this area?

CHIN YIN – NORTH-WEST FACING – RELATIONSHIPS AND MARRIAGE

Here you have your relationships, which are a yin enrichment, in the yin compass direction of north-west which is traditionally associated more with friendship than with romance. However, the friendships that come from this area can be far reaching and deep and they can last a lifetime. The ch'i here is expansive which can certainly expand those relationships into big events. Watch the ch'i doesn't become unpredictable sha though – this may make the relationships also unpredictable. Remedies here should include both sound and movement – a brightly painted wind chime perhaps?

CHIN TS'AI – WEST FACING – FRIENDS AND NEW BEGINNINGS

The ch'i here is changeable which can cause your friendships to blow hot and cold. And once the ch'i degrades it becomes dangerous and that could jeopardise friendships indeed. Remedy this area with both sound and stillness. If this area falls in a corner try propping up a beautiful, carved wooden flute and just see how it settles the ch'i.

CHANG YIN – SOUTH-WEST FACING – PLEASURE AND INDULGENCE

A nice yin enrichment facing the best yang direction it could – the ch'i here is soothing which couldn't be better for relaxing and indulging yourself. However, the ch'i can become disruptive sha and then you'll get no peace or quiet in this area. Who disrupts you here? Try remedying it with a combination of stillness and straight lines.

AN LU – SOUTH FACING – HEALTH AND PEACE

If you don't feel hale and hearty with this yang enrichment in such a vigorous yang compass direction then just maybe you are suffering from accelerating sha. Try remedying with a combination of straight lines and light.

*E*AST-FACING HOUSE – THE HOME OF THE SAGE

This is the home of someone with great wisdom and experience, only too happy to pass it on to others. This is the home of the teacher, the communicator, the lawyer, the trade union leader, the researcher, the pathologist. This is a yang house of someone who likes being out in the world but only to explore, to find out how the world works rather than to take from it.

WANG TS'AI – EAST FACING – FAME AND REPUTATION

When you step out of your front door into your fame area it is into the east, the traditional home of the benevolent Dragon who guides and offers great wisdom. And it is the same with the owner of this east-facing home. You have already gathered much wisdom and experience, and it is your role in life, as the wise sage, to pass that learning on to others who need it. Your reputation may well be, as is the ch'i from the east, growing. Caution should be exercised lest it becomes overpowering sha. This has the ability to sometimes cause people to forget that wisdom and experience belongs to the world from which it came – we have no personal claim to it – and as such we must maintain our humility. Fill this area with light and mechanical objects. The light should be subtle to ensure the ch'i remains at the right level and doesn't become too

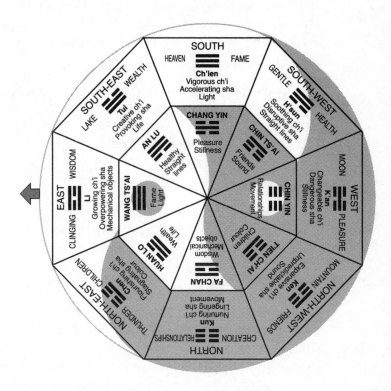

Figure 4.3 The east-facing house

overpowering. And the mechanical objects should reflect the teaching aspect of this area – calculators and computers perhaps.

HUAN LO – NORTH-EAST FACING – WEALTH AND POSSESSIONS

Here a typically yang enrichment enters a yin compass direction. This can cause problems if great wealth is sought after. However, the wealth enrichment may mean the wealth of learning that this house direction represents. Or it could be a wealth of compassion. The ch'i here is flourishing which means an accumulating wealth enrichment. The ch'i can become stagnating sha if the learning is not being passed on to enough people. Fill this area with colour and life. Plants with good strong colours would be appropriate – why not try amaryllis?

FA CHAN — NORTH FACING — WISDOM AND EXPERIENCE

Here your wisdom enrichment is in the north and would benefit from the help of your loved one. Why try to do everything alone? If your chosen path in life takes you out into the world you need the nurturing ch'i of the north to refresh and comfort you on your return. Here there could be a soul mate who would not only help you but also understand you. This is a good balance of a yang enrichment in a yin compass direction. This might be the perfect place to be. Watch the ch'i doesn't linger or you could find your relationship becoming one of pupil and teacher instead of two equals. Fill this area with moving mechanical objects.

T'IEN CH'AI — NORTH-WEST FACING — CHILDREN AND FAMILY

If you want your parenting to be relaxed and happy then you couldn't choose a better direction to be in. The expansive ch'i here from the north-west will ensure your children are your friends – and there'll be lots of them for you to enjoy. The ch'i here could become unpredictable if left unattended; make sure this area has lots of sound and colour. If it's full of children then I'm sure it will be anyway.

CHIN YIN — WEST FACING — RELATIONSHIPS AND MARRIAGE

A yin enrichment in a yin compass direction ought to provide you with good beneficial ch'i but it is changeable – coming from the White Tiger. It can quickly become dangerous sha. Your relationships in this area will never be dull. There's excitement, noise and fire here. If that's what you want and need then you will never be bored. If it's all too much then fill this area with stillness and movement in equal quantities. You need the serenity of a beautiful still statue that represents great movement in real life.

CHIN TS'AI – SOUTH-WEST FACING – FRIENDS AND
NEW BEGINNINGS

The south-west brings soothing gentle ch'i which will help
your friends bring you great peace of mind. The ch'i can
become disruptive sha so be prepared to use sound and
straight lines in this area. Pan pipes? Flutes?

CHANG YIN – SOUTH FACING – PLEASURE AND INDULGENCE

Wow, you like to live dangerously, don't you? How can you
relax with all that vigorous southern ch'i flooding in? Not
unless you like laying on the lawn in high summer listening
to the clack of croquet mallets and the tinkling of ice in tall
glasses of summer drinks. The ch'i can become accelerating
here which can exhaust you. Deflect it with stillness and
light. How about a large mirror facing outwards to channel
the ch'i back to where it is rushing from? Or at least turn it
aside before it totally drains you?

AN LU – SOUTH-EAST FACING – HEALTH AND PEACE

This is a good yang enrichment in a good yang location.
Here your health is benefiting from creative ch'i and should
bring you joy. If you feel provoked by the sha fill this area
with life and straight lines. You could cover your window
sills in pots all arranged in straight lines – and enjoy the
colour of summer plants or spring herbs. Or how about an
ant farm?

*S*OUTH-WEST-FACING HOUSE – THE HOME OF THE HEALER

This is the house of someone who uses intuitive healing
abilities to help others – the healer, the doctor, the nurse,
the counsellor, the astrologer, the clairvoyant. This is a good
yang direction for someone who likes to be out in the world
in a gentle way. Someone who can pass through this world
with great worth and yet never really touched by the world.

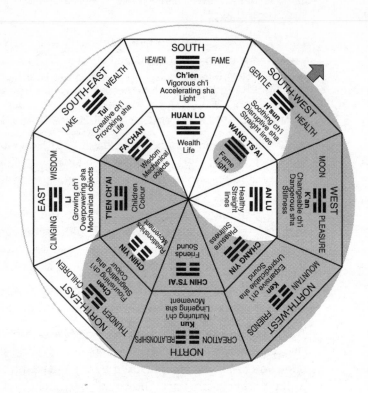

Figure 4.4 The south-west-facing house

WANG TS'AI – SOUTH-WEST FACING – FAME AND REPUTATION

Being out in the world is fine for the owner of this yang house, just so long as he or she can set the pace, choose the style of going which invariably will be gentle and soft. This is the most yin of the four yang directions. When you step out into the world you step out into the soothing wind of the south-west and you find your fame helping others overcome their difficulties which will probably be to do with their health – and that can be physical, emotional, or even spiritual. You can be their healer. Watch the ch'i doesn't become disruptive. To be of service you have to stay out of the way and allow that soothing ch'i to work through you – not because of you. If the ch'i becomes disruptive sha you will have to fill this area with light and straight lines. Here you can use lots of mirrors. Face them outwards to ward off the disruptive sha.

HUAN LO – SOUTH FACING – WEALTH AND POSSESSIONS

The south is known as the creative heaven direction, full of invigorating ch'i. What does this suggest to you? If you put yourself at the disposal of the ch'i and allow it to work through you for the greater good of everyone then only richness and abundance can flow your way. If the ch'i shows any tendency to become accelerating sha – and you can tell if it has become so from the amount of clutter you keep in this area – then remedy it with life and light. Plants with mirrors, well-lit aquariums, soft reading lamps and you could incorporate the red of the south with the plants – try geraniums in pots on the window sills to maximise the light and the life.

FA CHAN – SOUTH-EAST FACING – WISDOM AND EXPERIENCE

This is a good yang enrichment in a good yang compass direction. Here your wisdom can benefit from creative ch'i. You can learn and find new ways of putting that new wisdom to good effect. This may be something only you can do – lateral thinking. Taking the old ways and reworking them so that they become useful again. If the ch'i becomes provoking sha you will have to find ways to tone down your views – perhaps by filling this area with plants and a mechanical object that reflects a traditional task; if you have an open fire in this area a good, old-fashioned set of fire tongs or bellows would be good. Any plant with silver leaves would benefit you in this area.

T'IEN CH'AI – EAST FACING – CHILDREN AND FAMILY

This is a yin enrichment in a yang compass direction – the

balance, however, is good with your family benefiting from
growing ch'i from the benevolent wisdom of the Dragon.
The ch'i can become overpowering sha which can cause
your offspring to cling too much to you, and make it
difficult for you to find any freedom. You may feel
restricted. If this is the case fill this area with bright,
colourful, mechanical objects. How about a good visual
screen-saver if you keep a computer in this area? Or if this is
your kitchen you could have very brightly coloured pots
and pans.

CHIN YIN — NORTH-EAST FACING — RELATIONSHIPS
AND MARRIAGE

Here your relationships are benefiting from flourishing ch'i
which can be arousing and, at times, seem stormy and not
very productive. But this is only because the ch'i can
stagnate very easily. All you have to do is stir it up with lots
of colour and movement. Brightly coloured wind chimes in
this area will help. Or you could use crystals hanging in the
window to throw beams of coloured light around the room.

CHIN TS'AI — NORTH FACING — FRIENDS AND
NEW BEGINNINGS

Here your friendships benefit from nurturing ch'i. Any
friendships forged here will last a long time. This is a good
yin enrichment in the best yin compass direction for
protection and caring. If the ch'i becomes lingering you can
help it along with movement and sound. A good place to
play those old vinyl LPs to your friends over a good meal
and a late evening spent chatting and reminiscing.

CHANG YIN — NORTH-WEST FACING — PLEASURE AND INDULGENCE

Here your pleasure enjoys expansive ch'i. When things are
going right for you it's difficult to get the smile off your
face. What a good place to relax in and enjoy being you.
This is also a good place for the friends from Chin Ts'ai to
overspill and help you enjoy your leisure time. If the ch'i

becomes unpredictable sha you can make it more harmonious by using sound and stillness. How about hanging up a huge gong which you could bang when the discussions get too noisy or out of hand.

AN LU — WEST FACING — HEALTH AND PEACE

You, of all people, should know that stress can lead to all sorts of problems. Here the ch'i is changeable and needs to be watched carefully. This is a yang enrichment in a volatile yin compass direction. The power of the Tiger can be unleashed suddenly and unpredictably and become dangerous sha all too easily. This area needs straight lines which run at right angles away from the west (i.e. north to south) as well as stillness. How about a big, carved, wooden box filled with all the tools of your trade?

THE FOUR YIN DIRECTION HOUSES

NORTH-FACING HOUSE –
THE GREAT LOVER'S HOME

This is Don Juan's house. Or is it Casanova's? It doesn't matter: this is the house of the Great Lover. This is the house where the best, most romantic love songs are written, or the best romantic poetry is composed. I bet Browning lived in a north-facing house. As probably did Rupert Brooke when he wrote 'Breathless we flung us on the windy hill; laughed in the sun and kissed the lovely grass'. What a marvellous place to have your fame enrichment – your loved ones must know you to be the most caring, sensitive and considerate lover there is.

WANG TS'AI — NORTH FACING — FAME AND REPUTATION

This is where you are in the world – stepping out with your loved one on your arm. Don't you just feel that everything is right with the world when you are in love? Here all that

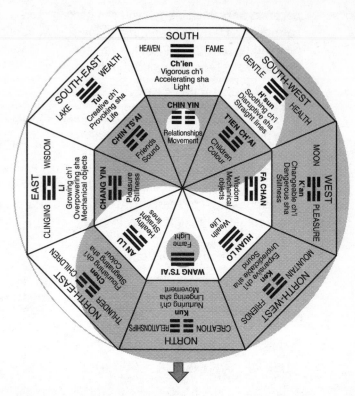

Figure 4.5 The north-facing house

nurturing north ch'i from the Black Tortoise is directed towards affairs of the heart – and quite rightly so. This is the most yang of enrichments in the most yin of compass directions, and it can quite turn our heads. If the ch'i becomes lingering sha then that's exactly what we do – linger: dwell on past hurts and mistakes. To remedy this all we have to do is fill this area with movement and light. Hang a small revolving mirror in your window and watch the light spin. Or, as this is a very watery location, you could do no better than an open fire. It will drive out the damp of a broken heart as well as providing the light and movement. Don't be fooled into thinking you can get away with an electric heater here – you can't. You need the flames.

Here a beam over a bed has been remedied with a mosquito net to slow the ch'i down.

An ideal south-facing view from a front door – the ch'i is invigorating from this direction.

A 'dead' corner can be remedied with light and mirrors. You can use candles or a lamp – or both.

Stillness remedy with a mirror to reflect the ch'i back into the room.

A west-facing window needs a plant remedy – here a clever idea has been to utilise a model greenhouse to effect the remedy.

The ch'i coming in from an overly large window can be remedied with a wooden slatted blind – and a cat as a life remedy of course.

You don't need mirrors to remedy a kitchen – you could use reflective surfaces such as stainless steel, as in this kitchen.

A perfect feng shui chair – curving, made of natural materials, comfortable, harmonious and inviting for 'honoured guest position'.

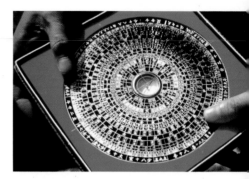

A feng shui compass, the lo p'an, being used by a consultant. Photo courtesy of the Hong Kong Tourist Association.

Two remedies used in conjunction – light and stillness. You can combine various remedies depending on the compass directions and enrichment being corrected.

An overly wide staircase with plants and mirror remedies to slow the ch'i down and stop it from rushing up too quickly.

An office desk and chair with its back to the door. How would you remedy this?

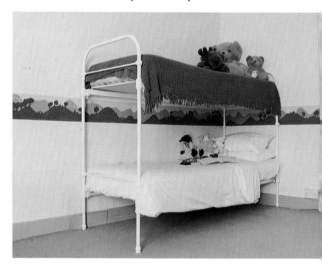

The 'dead' area under the top of children's bunk beds has been cleverly remedied with a frieze that channels the ch'i.

HUAN LO – NORTH-WEST FACING – WEALTH AND POSSESSIONS

Your finances will grow and shrink with alarming monotony – and you'll have no control over any of it until you settle this area with life and sound. Play music here to your plants and, as they grow and thrive, so will your funds. Watch what you spend – it's all too easy to be reckless with money when you have a north-west facing wealth enrichment.

FA CHAN – WEST FACING – WISDOM AND EXPERIENCE

A yang enrichment in a changeable yin compass direction which can cause you to speak without thinking sometimes – and about subjects you know you don't know enough about. The Tao says that those who know say nothing. Couldn't you pretend sometimes? If you want to settle the sha here then use a mechanical object combined with a stillness remedy. How about an astrolabe? Or a beautiful old brass telescope? That would get them talking – and you wouldn't have to say a word.

T'IEN CH'AI – SOUTH-WEST FACING – CHILDREN AND FAMILY

You have the power to soothe all their fears and hurts away – but don't they drive you mad when they want to do their own thing? This area is all black and white, on or off. This is an area of angels and beasts. One minute everything is perfect and the next it's the end of the world. To pull the two extremes towards each other you could use straight lines and colour in this area. How about a painted frieze round the room? Or a row of brightly coloured books? Romantic poetry books, of course.

CHIN YIN – SOUTH FACING – RELATIONSHIPS AND MARRIAGE

The most yin enrichment in the most yang location. Here's the place for creative, vigorous relationships, indeed. When you're in love the whole world knows about it. But your interests can wane so quickly if the ch'i becomes accelerating sha – too much, too soon? Remedy this excess of energy by lots of light and movement. Hang up mirrors to spin and deflect the accelerating sha.

CHIN TS'AI – SOUTH-EAST FACING – FRIENDS AND NEW BEGINNINGS

Your friendships enjoy the creative ch'i from this compass direction – they'll always find new ways of cheering you up when your love has left you. And you enjoy their positive input. But if they provoke you, remedy this area with life and sound. Place your stereo speakers in amongst the pot plants and watch your plants thrive.

CHANG YIN – EAST FACING – PLEASURE AND INDULGENCE

Some people like to switch off when they relax and do nothing – but not you. You're always thinking, always planning. And you learn from these relaxing, thinking sessions, don't you? However, if you find it difficult to completely unwind then use this area to contemplate on a beautiful practical object – a large statue won't do, it must be of some use. Perhaps a museum piece of some sort – an antique clock with all the workings showing? Or an old-fashioned globe?

AN LU – NORTH-EAST FACING – HEALTH AND PEACE

If you can balance this yang enrichment with the yin flourishing ch'i you can only enjoy good health. But the ch'i can stagnate and you may find yourself depressed by it. Remedy it with colour and straight lines. Try big, bright paintings here. Or decorate the walls in modern designs with lots of vivid colour and great swathes of fabrics.

NORTH-EAST-FACING HOUSE – THE HOME OF THE CHARISMATIC LEADER

This is known in Chinese feng shui as the Dragon's lair house: the home of the dragon, indeed. And dragons can't help but give advice – it's what they're there for. This is the house of the managing director, the prime minister, the

company president, the authority on any subject, the
barrister, the forensic scientist, the advertising executive,
the producer.

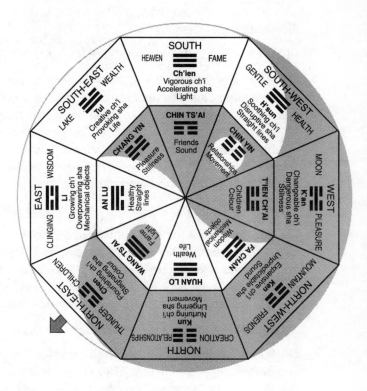

Figure 4.6 The north-east-facing house

WANG TS'AI – NORTH-EAST FACING – FAME AND REPUTATION

This is the enrichment where you step out into the world –
and your world is populated with lots of people seeking
advice, help, leadership, and your time and attention. You
flourish here. Being in charge comes so naturally to you that
others automatically accept you as the group leader – and
quite rightly so. Dragons actually know what they are

95

doing, even if they appear to be doing nothing at times. If the ch'i here stagnates too much, you may actually be doing nothing. Enliven it with light and colour. This area benefits from lots of bright green – try a reading lamp with a vivid, emerald green shade made of glass to let the light illuminate the whole room.

HUAN LO – NORTH FACING – WEALTH AND POSSESSIONS

One of your great dislikes is listening to advice from others. But if you don't learn to trust someone close to you then you will never make money – or hold on to your Dragon's gold hoard. You, as a Dragon, should know you have to nurture wealth. But you also have to learn how to spend it. Fill this area with life and movement if you want the lingering sha to return to being nurturing.

FA CHAN – NORTH-WEST FACING – WISDOM AND EXPERIENCE

Not a brilliant place for your humility to be allowed to show. Keep it simple. Keep it accurate and don't try to teach anyone anything unless they ask. Keep this area from becoming unpredictable by using sound and mechanical objects. Sounds to me like a CD player is needed here.

T'IEN CH'AI – WEST FACING – CHILDREN AND FAMILY

Oh, if only they would treat you with the respect you think you deserve. Well, they won't. They like provoking the Dragon and making it roar. And what better place to do it than in the opposite location for it to feel any peace. It's all too dark here, too 'feelie', too yin. Dragons like light and facts. Remedy this area with colour and stillness. One perfect brush stroke of colour on one perfect piece of driftwood should do it. Watch the west, it's a bad direction for Dragons.

CHIN YIN – SOUTH-WEST FACING – RELATIONSHIPS AND MARRIAGE

Here you can be soothed by all that south-west ch'i. This is a good yin enrichment in a gentle yang location. Your relationships may well benefit from being work partnerships as well – or at least someone in the background to stop you becoming too pompous. If the ch'i becomes disruptive sha, and no one likes being left alone more than you, remedy it and provide yourself with a more peaceful relationship by adding movement and straight lines; if you could incorporate a small fountain into this area that would be absolutely perfect. If you can't, then one of those huge musical chimes with long metal pipes will help.

CHIN TS'AI – SOUTH FACING – FRIENDS AND NEW BEGINNINGS

What a good place to have your friends enrichment. It's a good yin enrichment in a very positive yang location. Here your friends, and new beginnings of course, can benefit from all that positive vigorous ch'i. Here your friends can help you be creative. This is also a good location for anyone who works with a group or a team – together you can accomplish so much more than you could on your own – although you'll have to be the adviser to the team, of course. If anyone tries to hurry you too much then the ch'i has become accelerating sha and you'll need to slow it down by using light remedies and sound remedies. Place small mirrors facing outwards to deflect the sha and hang wind chimes on the outsides of the windows to catch the breeze and calm things down – this will give you space and time.

CHANG YIN – SOUTH-EAST FACING – PLEASURE AND INDULGENCE

This is the place in which you should be to relax and unwind. What have you got here? Is this area benefiting from all that creative ch'i? Or is it being wasted? Is this an area that provokes you, won't let you rest here? Then remedy it with lots of plants and beautiful statues. This is a good place to have a conservatory – one of those old Victorian-style conservatories with huge ferns and white marble busts.

AN LU – EAST-FACING – HEALTH AND PEACE

The ch'i here is growing – and it comes from the east, the spring. This is excellent for your health. You can recover quickly, improve your stamina and maintain good all-round health here. If the ch'i becomes overpowering sha you may be tempted to take on too much and exhaust yourself. Remedy this by incorporating a mechanical object with lots of straight edges into this area.

NORTH-WEST-FACING HOUSE – THE HOME OF THE PROTECTOR

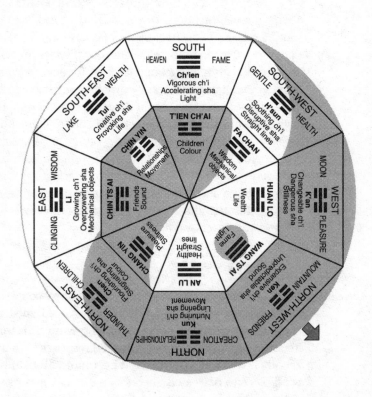

Figure 4.7 The north-west-facing house

This is the house of someone who looks out for others – this is the protector. You like to be the guardian of those who are perhaps weaker or in need of care. This is the house of the policeman, the critic, the priest, the charity worker, the judge, the social worker, the community worker.

WANG TS'AI – NORTH-WEST FACING – FAME AND REPUTATION

When you step out of your front door you step into the north-west – this is the compass direction of the Dog in Chinese astrology – and what better animal could there be to represent the great protector? The north-west is all to do with looking after other people, guarding them, not in a healing way but as a sort of emotional bodyguard, a spiritual minder. This is the home of someone who likes straight talking, a no-nonsense sort of person, great in a crisis, thoughtful and organised. You benefit from the expansive ch'i generated here and are popular and well liked when you're out in the world. If the ch'i becomes unpredictable sha and you find yourself getting 'snappy' then remedy this area with light and sound. Lots of good lamps and loud music should do it.

HUAN LO – WEST FACING – WEALTH AND POSSESSIONS

Your finances, facing in this direction, must be so changeable you wonder if you'll ever be straight moneywise. You may well have known such extremes as bankruptcy and 'rolling in it' – and it will keep changing so enjoy it while you have it and economise when you don't. If your finances ever look like becoming a severe problem then the ch'i has become dangerous sha and you'll need to fill this area with lots of plants, fish, cats – and dogs, of course. And when you do have some money about your person invest in one piece of perfect, exquisite fine art and keep it in this area – and don't be tempted to sell it when your finances take another dive – that'll only make things worse again.

FA CHAN — SOUTH-WEST FACING — WISDOM AND EXPERIENCE

At least you learn from your mistakes – unlike some other people. You like travel and learning about other cultures and this is a good yang enrichment in a good yang location. Enjoy the soothing ch'i when you need to learn more. If the ch'i becomes disruptive sha then remedy this area with straight lines and mechanical objects – sounds like a good place for a workshop or craft studio – or even an office with a computer and desk. Here you can surf the Net to your heart's content and explore the world you love so much.

T'IEN CH'AI — SOUTH FACING — CHILDREN AND FAMILY

Perfect place for a parent to be. You have limitless energy and great skill at entertaining small people. You delight in small children and find all that vigorous ch'i stimulating and rewarding. If it does become accelerating sha, which is probably rare, you may find yourself exhausted, so remedy it with lots of colour and light in this area. Lots of dark reds and greens, lots of mirrors, lamps and clean windows with the curtains pulled well back.

CHIN YIN — SOUTH-EAST FACING — RELATIONSHIPS AND MARRIAGE

A good yin enrichment that benefits from the creative ch'i of a yang location. This provides partnerships that are long term and reliable; relationships that bring you great joy and in which you find companionship and equality. You work well in a relationship although you are capable of being on your own without it bothering you too much – but it's in a relationship that you function better. If the relationship becomes provoking then remedy this area with lots of plants to calm the sha and lots of movement to encourage the ch'i to return to its creativity.

CHIN TS'AI — EAST FACING — FRIENDS AND NEW BEGINNINGS

It doesn't take you long to bounce back from adversity, nor does it take you long to make new friends and settle into new situations. You are a born mixer, and with all the growing ch'i from the east bringing you great experience to share with others you can't go wrong – not unless you allow the ch'i to become overpowering. In which case, remedy this area with mechanical objects and sound. How about learning a foreign language at home on cassette?

CHANG YIN – NORTH-EAST FACING – PLEASURE AND INDULGENCE

Here you can relax in warmth and comfort: a good yin enrichment in a good yin location. This area should be full of dark colours and rich fabrics. This should be a den to crawl into and lick your wounds, if you ever need such a place. The ch'i here is flourishing and you should be able to relax easily. If the ch'i becomes stagnating sha you may find yourself dwelling on past mistakes so remedy it with lots of colour and stillness. How about some modern art? Lots of bright brash colours will bring out the best in you.

AN LU – NORTH FACING – HEALTH AND PEACE

You may well be prone to injury – only because you rush at everything so eagerly. This enrichment is a good place to recuperate, it's quiet and yin, nurturing ch'i to heal and help you. If you find you spend too much time here, though, the ch'i has become lingering sha and you will need to remedy it with movement and straight lines. Lots of wind chimes to drive you back out into the world.

WEST-FACING HOUSE – THE HOME OF THE SOCIALITE

This is it, this is the one to which I want to be invited to supper. This is the house of the great cook, the chef, the wine connoisseur, the culinary writer, the farmer, the restaurant owner, the party thrower, the socialite, the decadent, stylish rogue who just loves to organise dinner parties. Yes, I would love to come.

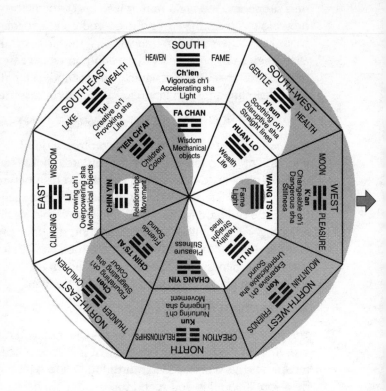

Figure 4.8 The west-facing house

WANG TS'AI – WEST FACING – FAME AND REPUTATION

As you step out of your front door you step into the great pleasure area of life. Not for you fame and fortune, oh, no. What you seek is culinary perfection, richness of taste, and exquisite menus and company to dine with. You can make your career in any industry that deals with food – just so long as it's the top-end of the market – or writing about food, or photographing it, or preparing it, cooking it, eating it – or just thinking about it. This is the location of changeable ch'i which means you like variety. You enjoy the richness that this world can offer – good food, wine, cars, furnishings and lifestyles. And why not indeed? Not many people can cope with a west-facing house – it's all too much for them and the ch'i becomes dangerous sha. If there's any likelihood of this happening to you, make sure you fill this area with light and stillness. The perfect candelabra set on a perfectly laid table? I wonder?

HUAN LO – SOUTH-WEST FACING – WEALTH AND POSSESSIONS

Too much wealth would unsettle you, despite what you think. Much better to slowly build up, to be comfortable rather than stinking rich – but you do need funds to pay for your decadent lifestyle. This south-west wealth enrichment will bring you enough but not too much. The ch'i here soothes rather than inflates. Should it degrade to sha it will be disruptive and you may find your finances cause you more problems than you anticipate. Remedy this area with lots of life and straight lines. Could be an aquarium? Better still, a fish farm.

FA CHAN – SOUTH FACING – WISDOM AND EXPERIENCE

Your wisdom enrichment is in the south which is the most yang of yang locations. Are you sure you know your subject well enough? We get the most vigorous ch'i from here, and it can overwhelm us if we are not sure enough of our ground. You may be a founder member of the bluffer's club, but learning is something that has to be ongoing. If the ch'i is allowed to become accelerating sha you will be tested – and may be found wanting. Study more and fill this area with light and mechanical objects. That certainly sounds like a computer to me.

T'IEN CH'AI – SOUTH-EAST FACING – CHILDREN AND FAMILY

Good place to be if you like children – and something tells me you certainly do otherwise you wouldn't have chosen a west-facing house. Children will bring you joy. They're your visible sign of creation and you find them stimulating and

103

enjoyable. They may provoke you, though, with their messy habits – so remedy this provoking sha with lots of plants (up high out of children's reach, of course) and lots of colour. You can forget about style and elegance in this area – fill it with dayglo, plastic, tacky – and you'll hate it and love it.

CHIN YIN — EAST FACING — RELATIONSHIPS AND MARRIAGE

The strongest yin enrichment in a yang location, known to the Chinese as 'the Clinging'. What does that tell you? If you enjoy and learn from growing within a relationship then this is a good area for you. If, however, you find it overpowering and find yourself overwhelmed with the need to escape then fill this area with movement and mechanical objects. The movement should be you – and the mechanical objects should be tools of your trade. This is a brilliant location to have your kitchen – but you have to learn to share it, don't you?

CHIN TS'AI — NORTH-EAST FACING — FRIENDS AND NEW BEGINNINGS

A perfect place for you. This is the place to entertain all those friends of yours. Good place for your dining room – and it could be next to the kitchen. It enjoys flourishing ch'i which is ideal for long dinner parties, fabulous Sunday lunches, storing fine wines and generally entertaining. This is the host's perfect place to be the perfect host. The ch'i could become stagnating sha, though – you'll have to change your menus and remedy this area with colour and sound. White can be a colour and the sound of laughter and conversation should do for the sound remedy.

CHANG YIN — NORTH FACING — PLEASURE AND INDULGENCE

If you've got your kitchen in the east and your dining room in the north-east then what could be better than your sitting room next. Here, in the north, you can relax after supper. Kick your shoes off and enjoy your coffee: you've probably earned it. This location is very yin, nurturing and warm, and here you can unwind. Great place to relax and spend the winter – lots of open fires and thick rugs, rich furnishings and comfortable chairs. If the ch'i is allowed to linger here you'll never move. Remedies are to have movement and stillness. This may sound like a contradiction but you could try an open fire surrounded by a beautiful, ornate fireplace.

AN LU – NORTH-WEST FACING – HEALTH AND PEACE

The only advice that is associated with this area is to watch your weight. The ch'i here is expansive and so could you too expand. To remedy this fill this area with sound and straight lines. This may be a good place to keep the logs for the open fire. The sound could be you chopping wood and containing that expansive ch'i. If it's allowed to become unpredictable sha, who knows what could happen? It's unpredictable.

FINDING THE MISSING PIECES

Now we've looked at the different directions your house could face we have to look at which bits of your house are missing. First, you need a ground plan of your house. This could be a simple sketch, a rough outline; it doesn't have to be anything too elaborate. Once you have a ground plan you can overlay the Pah Kwa on to it. If your house is roughly a square shape, the Pah Kwa will cover the outline of the house. But what if your house is 'L' shaped? Or very long and thin? Well, when you've overlaid the Pah Kwa on to the ground plan, you'll find it doesn't fit without distorting it. What we are interested in is which bits are missing – or which pieces do you have too much of?

Any extra bits of your house are enrichments that you have in abundance – perhaps too much abundance – only you can tell. Any bits that are missing are the enrichments you don't have. The enrichments should each occupy about an eighth part of your life if you are to have harmony and balance.

If you have any missing enrichments then you can hang large mirrors at the point where the enrichment should begin – this works for enrichments that are too small, as well. This will give the illusion of the enrichment being there – or being larger. And, hopefully, this will enhance that area of your life so that you benefit from the elements or qualities of that enrichment.

Any enrichments that are too large should be closed down by lowering the lighting levels, or you can restrict the ch'i by using straight-line remedies to stop the ch'i expanding in that area too much.

In Chapter 5 we will walk through your home and look at each room in detail.

5

FENG SHUI
IN THE HOME

I will arise and go now, and go to Innisfree,
And a small cabin build there, of clay and wattles made:
Nine bean-rows will I have there, a hive for the honey-bee,
And live alone in the bee-loud glade.
And I shall have some peace there, for peace comes dropping slow,
Dropping from the veils of the morning to where the cricket sings;
There midnight's all a-glimmer, and noon a purple glow,
And evening full of the linnet's wings.
I will arise and go now, for always night and day
I hear the lake water lapping with low sounds by the shore;
While I stand on the roadway, or on the pavements gray,
I hear it in the deep heart's core.

W. B. YEATS

We've already looked at the basic principles of feng shui in the home in Chapter 4. You've drawn up a plan of your house or apartment and overlaid the Pah Kwa on to it, so you know in which enrichment each of the rooms in your house falls. You've checked to see where you need remedies to make sure that each of these areas enrich your life as much as they should. And you've applied the remedies that are appropriate to that enrichment, or to the direction in which the room faces. So what else is there?

As well as these general considerations, there are certain feng shui principles that are specific to particular rooms or parts of the house, and that's what this chapter is about. And you'll see that some of these require specific remedies regardless of which part of the house the room is in. So let's

107

go round the house room by room, and see what further improvements you can make.

FRONT DOOR

This seems like a good place to start. We've already discussed the view from your front door; this will largely determine what sort of ch'i is entering the house. In Chapter 6 we'll look at how you can influence the ch'i as it flows through your front garden to the door. This will be a factor in whether you need to apply further remedies to improve the ch'i. If the view is good – especially if it's south facing – and you have a front garden and have maximised the positive ch'i flowing through it, you may not need to apply further remedies. But if you have a poor view, and especially if you have no front garden, you will need to do what you can to improve the ch'i as it reaches the door. It's very important, after all, to make sure that the ch'i is as beneficial as possible before it ever enters the house.

So what can you do if a remedy is needed? You can use any remedy, although the one that is appropriate to the relevant enrichment or direction is ideal. If you need a light remedy, put a glass panel in the door. Or you could paint it a bright, cheerful colour for a colour remedy. Or combine the two and change the door for one with stained-glass panels. The colour you paint the front door should be influenced by the direction it faces:

- **South or south-east** (fire) – red, purple, orange and strong, bright yellow are fire colours. If the ch'i is too strong, use a green, wood shade.
- **North** (water) – blue and black are the classic water colours, but you can use the metal colours of white or gold.
- **East or north-east** (wood) – the wood colour is

green, but you can use the water colours of blue and
black.

 West or north west (metal) – gold or white are the
ideal colours or, if the ch'i is too strong, use brown or
yellow, earth colours.

 South-west (earth) – the earthy browns and yellows
are ideal here, but you can use the fire colours, red,
orange, strong yellow or purple.

The pattern of any decoration or panelling on the front
door is important. If it is made of vertical timber planking,
you have a straight line remedy. A round or octagonal
window let into the door will help the ch'i to flow
harmoniously.

The next thing to consider is the size of the front door. Is it
in proportion to the entrance hall? If it's too large, there's a
danger that the ch'i will all flow out. You can encourage it
to stay in the hall by hanging a wind chime just inside the
door. What if the door is too small? In this case you can
hang mirrors in the hall to reflect the door and make it
appear bigger.

The area around the front door, both inside and outside,
should be kept tidy and free of clutter. The door and the
door frame are crucial to the well-being of the entire
household. It is important to keep them in good condition,
regularly painted and free from damage or rot. Have a light
– or maybe two – outside the door to welcome visitors; be
sure to replace any bulbs promptly if they blow or the ch'i
will be discouraged.

ENTRANCE HALL

The ch'i that circulates around your house has to pass
through the entrance hall on its way in and out. How do
you think it responds? Is it encouraged to linger, does it
rush out of the door, or does it stagnate?

One of the most important factors is the staircase, if you have one. If this faces the front door the ch'i can rush straight down it and out of the door without pausing, taking your energy, your luck and your money with it. This is emphasised if the stairs are a straight run with no bends. The solution is to hang a wind chime above the bottom of the stairs to slow the ch'i down. If there is room, you could block the ch'i with a screen between the bottom of the stairs and the door. Failing that, raise the threshold so you have to take a step up to go out through your front door. This is also a useful remedy if your door opens on to a flight of steps outside it.

It's good news if there are windows in your entrance hall; these encourage ch'i to circulate harmoniously. If you have no windows in your hall – perhaps you live in an apartment – use mirrors to reflect windows from neighbouring rooms and leave a door open to let additional light in.

SITTING ROOM

Which way does your sitting room face? How can you tell? Windows are the eyes through which a room looks out, so it is reckoned to face whichever way the windows face. If you have a room without windows, the Chinese say that the room is 'blind', and has bad feng shui. However, you can remedy this with mirrors, which represent windows; if there are no windows the room faces the direction on to which the door opens. If there are windows on two or more sides you should be able to tell intuitively which way the room faces – one side will have larger windows, or a longer view, or something that gives you a feel for which way it faces. A room with windows on the south and east sides is considered extremely lucky.

You need to establish which way the room faces, and which enrichment it falls into; this will tell you which remedies are the best here. Hopefully, the sitting room will be in an appropriate enrichment such as pleasure or friends. If not, and you can't rearrange the rooms in the house, introduce remedies that are apt for the enrichments in which you would like the room to fall. For example, stillness is the best remedy in your pleasure enrichment, so introduce stillness to your sitting room. Or introduce sound to bring the benefits of the friends enrichment, which is associated with sound remedies.

The most important seat in the sitting room is known as 'honoured guest position'; this is the chair that faces the door and should be the most comfortable seat in the room. You can tell which chair it is because it's the one you always choose to sit in yourself – if you can get there before anyone else.

Honoured guest position

The rest of the seating should be arranged to form an octagon incorporating the 'honoured guest' seat. It isn't necessary, especially in a small room, to fill in all eight sides, but you should position the furniture to fill in at least some of the sides. With four or fewer chairs and sofas, these should be placed at right angles to each other to form two, three or four sides of a square. If you have more seats, use these to fill in the 'corner' positions. You can also fill in these corner positions with coffee tables (see Figures 5.1 and 5.2).

You should always position a large coffee table in the centre of the seating area. This represents the central location of the earth element, and should be a regular shape: circular, square or rectangular.

Focal points

The focal point of the sitting room is traditionally the fireplace. This can create one of the eight sides of the octagon, with the seating grouped around it. However, the

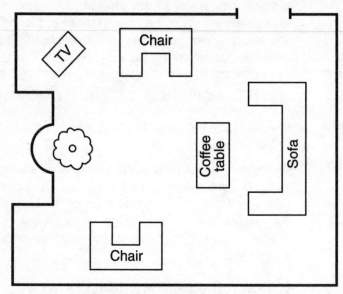

Figure 5.1 Sitting room before rearrangement

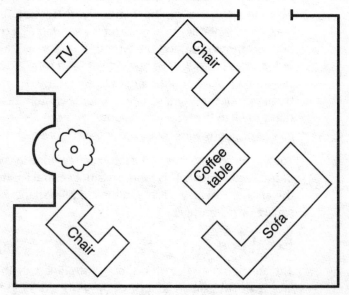

Figure 5.2 Sitting room with Pah Kwa furniture arrangement

seats should not be clustered too closely around it. If the room is large, place a mirror over the fireplace to bring in the area of the room outside the seating, and bring the ch'i along with it.

Nowadays, the focal point may be the television rather than the fireplace. If this is the case, try to site it on the east side of the room, since it is a mechanical device. If this isn't possible, site it in the north, north-east or north-west. Avoid putting it on the west side of the room, and wherever you put it, aim to hide or screen it in some way when it isn't being used.

Remember that ch'i hates clutter. This can be difficult, especially with a small room, as sitting rooms tend to collect ever-increasing piles of magazines, children's toys, address books, television remote controls, used shopping lists and other accumulated bits and pieces. But do try to keep it as clear as possible, and what you can't keep clear, at least keep tidy. This is different from keeping the room empty. It should be warm and comfortable with ornaments, and pictures on the walls – but not cluttered.

Dead areas

Alcoves and dead corners are bad for the flow of ch'i; you can use a remedy to bring them into the room. Pot plants are useful for this purpose, but make sure you use plants with rounded leaves. A side-light will also help to bring a dead area to life. Corners jutting into the room also need to be remedied, and plants are useful for this. Use either a tall plant or a trailing plant placed on a high shelf.

Colour scheme

The colour scheme of the room should suit the direction it faces:

- ☺ **South** – reds and oranges
- ☺ **South-east** – reds, terracotta and yellows

- **East** – strong greens
- **North-east** – soft greens
- **North** – blues
- **North-west** – off white shades
- **West** – white, with gold highlights
- **South-west** – browns, yellows or natural shades.

KITCHEN

The Chinese word for wealth sounds the same as the word for food. The better you eat, the healthier you are. And the healthier you are, the better able you are to earn money. So the kitchen is associated with wealth. If you have a choice, situate it in your wealth enrichment. It is also very comfortable in the health enrichment, for obvious reasons.

The most important function of the kitchen is cooking. Traditionally, this was done over an open fire of bamboo or wood, so the kitchen is associated with the elements of wood and fire. This means that it is best situated in the south, south-east, east or north-east of the house.

The kitchen should be well lit and well ventilated. Use lights and mirrors to make sure that there are no dark corners, especially near the cooker. You can also use reflective surfaces such as stainless steel. When you are cooking in your kitchen, you should be able to see anyone entering the room, so island units for working at are very good. If you don't have room for an island unit, position mirrors so that you can see people entering.

Many kitchens have two doors – one leading into the rest of the house, and the other leading out into the back garden. If people are inclined to pass straight through the kitchen without stopping, on their way in or out of the back door, ch'i will do the same thing. So block its path and make it move round the room; put the kitchen table in the way, for example.

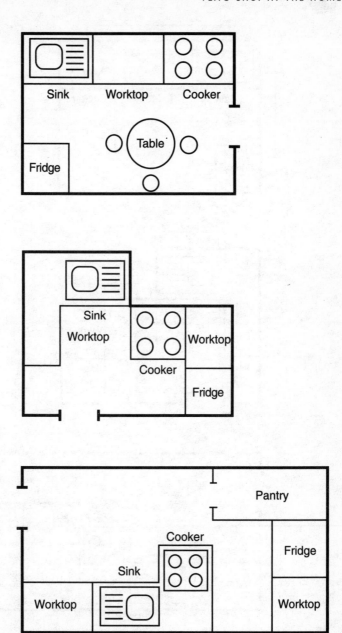

Figure 5.3 Three kitchen plans

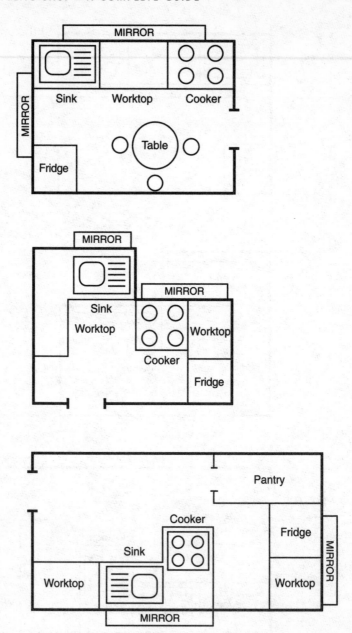

Figure 5.4 Three kitchens after re-design

The cooker should not be immediately next to the sink since the fire and water elements will clash; equally the cooker will not sit well next to the fridge. Make sure the cooker is kept clean and in proper working order all the time, as it is very bad luck for it to be dirty or broken. The fridge door shouldn't open towards the door of the kitchen because the cold fridge is yin, and people are yang.

DINING ROOM

As with the sitting room, the furniture should be arranged in the dining room to encourage the ch'i to flow harmoniously. The table itself should be round, oval or square. It can be rectangular but only if the rectangle is fairly short – long, thin tables are bad feng shui since they funnel the ch'i too strongly. As you will no doubt have guessed, octagonal tables are excellent for feng shui.

The table and chairs should not be too large for the room. If the door opens straight on to the chairs, or there is little room to fit comfortably round the table, the room is too cramped. It would be better to eat somewhere else or have a smaller table. If you like entertaining on a large scale, give your guests a buffet-style meal rather than trying to cram them all round the table.

The dining room shouldn't be too close to the front door – and the front door should never open straight on to it. Otherwise people will simply eat and leave. It should also not be too close to the toilet, as unhealthy ch'i may flow into it.

Try to avoid eating meals in the kitchen, as it is a very yang location, and the influence is too strong for an eating area. If the dining room leads off the kitchen, keep the interconnecting door closed while you are eating.

Mirrors in the dining room are very beneficial, since they make every meal seem larger, and therefore increase all its beneficial qualities – its healthiness and tastiness. Make sure that the mirrors are positioned where they reflect the food spread out on the table.

STUDY

The key piece of furniture in the study is the desk, so this should face the door. Never sit with your back to the door. Since studies tend to be used either for looking after your money – doing your accounts, paying your bills and so on – or for earning money, try to locate your study in the wealth enrichment.

The other use for home studies is for learning, in which case they are best in the wisdom area of the house. If the study is near the front door your money could escape out through it, so try to find somewhere else to work. If you really can't move it, at least make sure you always work with the door shut. The same applies if your study is upstairs facing the top of the staircase, where the money can run down the stairs and out of the door.

Studies at home are often incorporated into other rooms. This is fine so long as they are in a suitable enrichment. And make sure that within the room the study is also within the right enrichment. We've already established how you can tell which way a room faces; overlay the Pah Kwa on to it and calculate the enrichments within the room.

If your study doubles with another room make sure that the use of the room is well balanced between its two functions. Don't cram the study into a corner under the stairs, or into an alcove, since the ch'i can't circulate so well in these nooks and crannies. Make sure that the lighting in the room is equally spread between the study area and the rest of the room. Don't have a brightly lit study area on one side of a softly lit bedroom, for example.

BEDROOM

The feng shui of your bedroom is arguably more important than anywhere else in the house. After all, we spend about a third of our lives asleep. Find out which enrichment your bedroom falls in and, if it's not right for you, swap it with another room if you can. The best enrichments for a bedroom are relationships, pleasure or health. And try to use a bedroom that faces in a direction which is compatible with your personal element. At the very least, overlay the Pah Kwa on your bedroom only, and put the bed in the best possible direction and enrichment for the room.

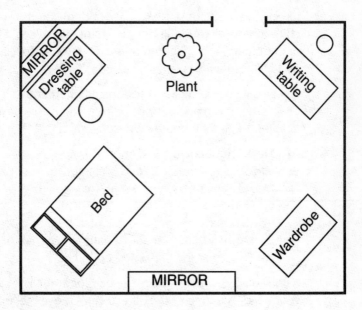

Figure 5.5 Bedroom furniture with Pah Kwa

The bed should be positioned somewhere which roughly faces the door, so that you can see people entering the room. However, it's not good to have the foot of the bed directly facing the door; this is the way that people are laid out when they die, before being carried out feet first. If you can't put the bed in a position from where the door is easily visible, hang a mirror so that when you are in bed you can see the door reflected in it.

If you have exposed beams in your bedroom, you don't want to place the bed underneath them. Whichever part of your body lies under the beam will suffer health problems. If the beam crosses over your head, you will suffer from headaches and insomnia; if it crosses the middle of your body you are likely to have stomach problems; and if it crosses above your legs you will be prone to complaints such as swollen ankles and water on the knee.

When it comes to the bed itself, make sure that it doesn't sit directly on the floor but has space underneath it so that the ch'i can flow all round and under you as you sleep. Those old-fashioned Victorian iron or brass beds are especially good, since they sit well off the floor.

It is best if your bed has a headboard, whether this is solid or whether it is made of brass or iron. Try to choose a headboard that suits your own element:

- **Fire:** bright colours and angular shapes
- **Wood:** square-shaped and preferably made of wood
- **Metal:** iron or brass or, failing that, coloured gold or white
- **Water:** curvy shapes and coloured blue or blue-green
- **Earth:** headboards made of natural materials or fabrics, in natural unpainted or undyed colours.

A light placed directly above the bed, or a wall light above your head, is bad feng shui. If you can't move the light, avoid switching it on and use table lights instead.

Children's bedrooms should be kept free from clutter (yes, I know it's not easy to persuade teenagers of this). Children with behavioural problems, or who are going through a difficult adolescence, will find life far easier if their bedrooms are kept clear. Televisions in the bedroom are a very bad idea; a television is a very strong mechanical device, which stirs up the ch'i in a room where you want to introduce calm and stillness while its occupants sleep. Removing the television can cause a dramatic and swift change for the better.

BATHROOM

The same rules apply in bathrooms as in other rooms. Make sure that you can see the door from both the bath and the lavatory, and if you are standing in front of the basin. If your back is to the door in any of these places, hang mirrors so that you can see the door reflected when you are in these positions.

It shouldn't be possible to see the lavatory as you first open the door so make sure it isn't facing the door. If this is unavoidable, distract anyone coming into the room by hanging a wind chime just inside the door. Always keep the bathroom door closed.

Bathrooms should be as spacious and uncluttered as possible. In order to maximise this, paint them in white or pale colours, and store as many items as possible inside cupboards rather than out on shelves.

Lavatory

If you leave the seat and lid of your lavatory up, the ch'i will disappear down the waste pipes along with the water. Water is associated with wealth, so if you let the ch'i out this way you'll be flushing your money away every time you

121

flush the lavatory. So it's very important that you always leave the seat and lid down. If you have a separate cloakroom keep the door to that closed as well.

STAIRS

Ch'i travels from floor to floor up and down the stairs, just as we do. So staircases are a very important consideration in feng shui. Staircases should be wide and brightly lit, and uncluttered. Don't keep piles of books or other objects on your stairs. Doors at the top or bottom of the stairs are obviously a bad idea, since they prevent the ch'i from moving between floors. Open-tread stairs encourage the ch'i to flow through rather than up them, so fresh ch'i doesn't reach the upstairs rooms and the ch'i that is up there stagnates.

Staircases that run straight with no bends in them can encourage the ch'i to flow too fast down them, so break them up by hanging wind chimes above the stairs. Stairs with too many bends in them, or too tight a bend, can restrict the flow of ch'i; if this is the case, hang mirrors on the bends to help the ch'i round the corners.

Spiral staircases have their own special problems. For one thing, they are usually open tread, letting the ch'i fall through. As well as this, they encourage the ch'i to spiral down helter-skelter and become accelerating sha. The solution is to slow the ch'i down by growing a climbing indoor plant up the banister rail or the central column. If this is impossible, give the impression of it by wrapping a green ribbon round the rails. If the staircase is an old-fashioned spiral stair in a turret, fix a rope banister against the outer wall in such a way that it hangs in gentle curves between each of the brackets that hold it to the wall.

CORRIDORS

Like staircases, corridors should be wide and well lit to encourage ch'i to flow smoothly along them. If they are narrow, add mirrors to make them appear wider. Keep them as well lit as you can, and make sure that at least some of the doors leading off corridors are kept open to let more light in to them (but not the toilet door). You can improve the view in a dark corridor or landing by placing a mirror to reflect a view from one of the neighbouring rooms.

Long corridors can funnel the ch'i too fast, so you'll need to break them up by hanging something from the ceiling such as wind chimes or banners. If the corridor is wide enough, you can put screens up that project into it to slow the ch'i down, or stand pots with tall plants in them against the walls.

A corridor that is very short can have the reverse effect by blocking ch'i and causing it to stagnate. If this is the case, hang a mirror at one or both ends of the corridor to give the impression of lengthening it.

DOORS

Doors should be hinged so that they open into the room, and on to the main area of the room. A door in the corner of a room which opens so that the first view is of the wall should be re-hung. If you are met by a view of a solid wall, so will the ch'i. It will stagnate, and your life – or at least the part of your life that correlates with the enrichment the door is in – will stultify along with it. It is almost as bad to have the door open straight on to a piece of furniture – try to keep the door area as clear as possible so the ch'i has a free passage.

As with the main front door, the size of the other doors in your house is also important: they should be in proportion to the room. If a door is too small, place mirrors to encourage the ch'i into the room. If it is too large, a wind chime will prevent the ch'i from rushing out of it.

Doors should be kept clean and in good condition, and they shouldn't jam as you open or close them. It should always be possible to close a door properly and to open it completely without its way being blocked.

The alignment of doors is also important. If two doors lead off a corridor or landing opposite each other, they must be *exactly* opposite. If they aren't, hang mirrors to reflect the section of each door that projects beyond the other door. If two opposite doors are different sizes, the larger door should lead to the more important room. If it doesn't – for example, the small door leads to the sitting room and the large door only to the cloakroom – hang a mirror on the large door so that the smaller door seems increased in size.

A door at the end of a long corridor will suffer because the ch'i will be funnelled too quickly into the room. Use a remedy in the corridor as we have already seen, but also hang a mirror on the outside of the door to avert some of the ch'i.

Doors that are too close together and open on to each other are very bad feng shui. Re-hang one of the doors, or replace it with narrower double doors that don't reach the second door. If the doorknobs of the two doors bang together when the doors are opened, this is even worse. The Chinese call it 'clashing teeth', and it causes conflict in the enrichment the doors are in. If you really can't change either door, at least move one of the doorknobs up or down.

WINDOWS

Do your windows open inwards or outwards? Or are they sash windows which slide up and down? Ideally, your windows should open outwards, letting in the maximum ch'i. If they open inwards, this is an introverted house and the ch'i may get trapped inside unless the windows are opened to their fullest extent. Windows that face west should definitely not open inwards, since they are inviting in unpredictable ch'i. If you can't re-hang the window, don't open it. In China, west-facing windows are often even boarded up to block out the light.

Sash windows never allow you to expose the entire window opening, since half of it (at least) always remains covered. If you cannot change the windows, however, you can ease the ch'i in and out by opening the top half and placing a pot plant on the windowsill. If you live in an old house, such as a Georgian house, which was built with sash windows originally, this is the option to go for. It would be a bad idea to change the windows since the house is older than you and the windows are a part of its character and personality – it would be bad feng shui to interfere with this. In any case, old Georgian houses tend to have large windows which minimises the problem of the ch'i being blocked as it flows through them.

Windows should always be set high enough so that the top of them is above the eye level of anyone living in the house, otherwise it can cause depression. When it comes to unusually shaped windows, round and octagonal windows are excellent, as are arched ones, but windows that come to a point at the top can disrupt the ch'i as it enters.

Windows should always be kept in good condition: make sure they don't stick when you open them, and repair any broken panes promptly.

CEILINGS

Ceilings should be reasonably high but not too high for the proportions of the room. If they are low, paint them white or pastel shades, and if they are too high, paint them a darker colour than the rest of the room. If you have a cornice running round the top of the walls this is ideal, since it prevents ch'i from getting stuck in the angle between the wall and the ceiling.

Sloping ceilings are fine so long as they don't come down below eye level. If they do, don't use the area beneath the slope for working, sitting or sleeping, but simply for storage or for placing decorative ornaments. These should be tall, thin shapes to make the height below the slope appear greater.

Exposed beams, which are very popular in the West, are frowned on by the Chinese. The ch'i can travel too fast along them and become accelerated. The remedy for this is to break them up by hanging wind chimes, banners or any other ornament from them. You can also use a straight-line remedy, especially in the south-west part of the house. To do this, take two straight objects, such as bamboo flutes, and place them against the beam at an angle of 45 degrees, so that one end points at the ceiling and the other at the wall. Place each one about a third of the way along the beam (one at each end). This cuts off the corner where the beam meets the wall, and – together with the walls – creates the top half of the Pah Kwa octagonal shape.

Beams are also considered oppressive, since they are load bearing. We have already seen that it is not good to sleep with a beam over the bed. Again, break up the beams with a wind chime or banner – the Chinese often tie red ribbons to them – and don't place any important furniture under them such as beds, desks, sofas and chairs, dining tables or cookers.

6

FENG SHUI
IN THE GARDEN

The leaves fall early this autumn, in wind.
The paired butterflies are already yellow with August
Over the grass in the West garden;
They hurt me. I grow older.
If you are coming down through the narrows of
  the river Kiang,
Please let me know beforehand,
And I will come out to meet you
As far as Cho-fu-sa.

EZRA POUND

The way that ch'i flows around your garden is just as important as the way it flows around the interior of your house. If you want a garden that brings you fun, relaxation or peace and quiet, you need to make sure that its feng shui is good. The feng shui of your garden is affected by its boundaries – fences, walls, hedges and so on – and by the paths, patios, ornaments and ponds within it. It is also influenced by any buildings, such as summerhouses, greenhouses or garden sheds, and, of course, by the trees, shrubs and flowers that are growing in it.

But before you consider any of that, what shape is your garden? If you could choose your garden, the best shape of all would be a garden that goes round all four sides of your house, creating a buffer zone between you and the outside world. That would allow you to control the ch'i entering your house from any direction. However, most of us don't get such a choice. Don't worry – you can still design good feng shui for a backyard, or even a window box. The principles are exactly the same.

GARDEN YIN AND YANG

Let's go back to that ideal south-facing house the Chinese traditionally say you should have (this is your cue to look smug if you actually have one). The nourishing yang ch'i from the south passes through your front garden on its way into your house. The front garden is a very yang area: it's open, public, expansive. It presents your face to the outside world. The back garden, on the other hand, faces north and is the private, protected area fed by the north's nurturing ch'i – a very yin kind of place to be.

Even if your house doesn't face south, the front garden is still a yang area and the back garden a yin area. You need to take this into account when you assess the feng shui of both gardens, and do what you can to encourage yang ch'i at the front by opening up the south aspect to let it in, and likewise encourage the nurturing ch'i of the north into your back garden to encourage its yin nature.

HOW MANY GARDENS?

The first thing to do is to overlay the Pah Kwa on to a plan of your garden. If you have separate front and back gardens, go through this exercise twice, once for each. If your front and back gardens join up round the side, use your judgement as to whether you have one garden or two. If they are joined by a narrow alleyway, you should probably treat them as two separate gardens. If they feel like one garden, treat them as one garden.

You'll have to decide for yourself whether to treat your garden as one or more sections if it's an unusual shape. You can also consider which you would like it to be. If you have garden on two sides of the house and you have chosen to divide them with a hedge or wall, you will probably regard them as two gardens for feng shui purposes. But if you choose to use them as a single open area, you should probably treat them as one for feng shui purposes.

Any garden that is on more than one side of the house, and is treated as one garden, is bound to have a chunk out of it when you overlay the Pah Kwa on to it. The house will be occupying at least one of the enrichments. This will affect the way you use the garden and what you can get out of it. For example, if the house occupies the pleasure and indulgence enrichment, you may find that you can't really relax and enjoy yourself in the garden – you're always mowing lawns or weeding or creosoting the fence. If your wealth enrichment is blocked, perhaps you never have enough money to make the changes you would like in the garden. Of course, this applies to gardens that have a chunk out of them for any reason, not just because the house is in the way.

WHICH WAY DOES THE GARDEN FACE?

In order to work out where the enrichments fall in your garden, you need to work out which way it faces. This depends on where the most commonly used entrance to it is. The front garden is the yang area – the public aspect of your garden – so it is reckoned to face in whichever direction people enter it from the outside world; the road or path outside the garden.

The back garden, being a yin area, belongs to the house, so it faces towards the entrance that you use yourself, which is most commonly the back door. But some gardens are not directly attached to the house, in which case the doorway or gate you enter it through is in the direction it faces. If you have a garden that leads off another one, and which you feel should be treated as a separate garden for feng shui purposes, again this is reckoned to face the entrance through which you most often reach it.

REMEDIES IN THE GARDEN

We've already looked at the eight remedies and how you use them in the house. The principles are exactly the same in the garden, but the actual remedies you use may be different. Electric lights are less often an option in the garden, for example, and I don't recommend you keep your computer out there. So let's go through the eight remedies again, and have a look at how you could use them in your garden.

LIGHT

You may be able to light up dark areas by using garden lights, but there are plenty of other options. The simplest is to prune or cut back plants to let more light into the area, but you could also use mirrors or a pond sited in such a way that it reflects light into the dark area. Or replant the area using plants with lighter coloured or less dense foliage. Use light as a remedy in the south and in your fame enrichment.

SOUND

Wind chimes are an obvious solution where you need a sound remedy, or you could use running water. As far as the Chinese are concerned, water is an essential element in even the smallest garden. Ch'i loves water – it encourages it to flow more smoothly; remember that feng shui means 'wind and water'. A stream or fountain, or a simple feature with water trickling over stones, will create beautiful sound remedies. Use sound as a remedy in the north-west and in your friends enrichment.

COLOUR

This is easy in a garden when the flowers are out, but it takes more careful planning to make sure that the colour remains all year. If you have difficulty achieving this with plants, try using coloured pots, ornaments or garden seats. Red is a particularly popular colour with the Chinese because it is vibrant and stimulates ch'i to flow. But if you need only a mild effect you can use milder shades, and remember that green is a colour. Use colour as a remedy in the north-east and in your children enrichment.

LIFE

Something alive can encourage ch'i into corners and crannies that it otherwise misses out. Obviously the plants in your garden are alive (at least, let's hope so!) so you could use them. But if you prefer, you can have a pond full of fish, which the Chinese would consider especially lucky. Or you can put a bird table in a dead space and watch the birds come to liven it up. Use life as a remedy in the south-east and in your wealth enrichment.

MOVEMENT

There are plenty of ways of bringing movement to a part of the garden that needs it. This is another opportunity for a bird table or moving water of some kind, such as a fountain. Or you can use wind chimes here. You could even plant something delicate that moves in the slightest breeze such as an aspen tree, or an ornamental grass with delicate fronds. Use movement as a remedy in the north and in your relationship enrichment.

STILLNESS

If you need to slow down ch'i try using a statue or a large urn. Some garden pots look beautiful if you leave them empty; if you choose to plant up a pot you are using as a stillness remedy, use a single plant that has a solid, simple shape, such as a clipped box tree or a yucca. Use stillness as a remedy in the west and in your pleasure enrichment.

MECHANICAL DEVICE

Any functional object that you use in the garden can help to stir up sluggish ch'i. Perhaps this is the place to keep the barbecue? Or you could put a sundial here, or the kids' garden swing. Use mechanical devices as a remedy in the east and in your wisdom enrichment.

STRAIGHT LINES

These can be either horizontal or vertical. Horizontal straight lines can be created with paths, or the edges of flower beds, or the beams across the top of a pergola. You can use arches to create vertical straight lines, or even beanpoles in the vegetable garden, or you can plant any plants with straight stems such as a standard rose. Use straight lines as a remedy in the south-west and in your health enrichment.

THE EIGHT ENRICHMENTS IN THE GARDEN

As with your house, once you have drawn a plan of your garden and overlaid the Pah Kwa on to it, you can see where each of your enrichments falls. Once again, you can see whether any are missing, and look at why and what the effect on your life might be as a result. This will differ subtly from the effect that missing the same enrichment from your house would have. The garden is outside your house and surrounds it. So the feng shui of your garden influences what is around you rather than influencing you, yourself. For example, improving the feng shui of the children enrichment of your house will improve the way you relate to your children, how you respond to them, how stressful you find parenthood and so on. The children enrichment of your garden, however, influences the way that your children respond to you. Clearly these are closely interrelated, but the distinction is important.

To give you another example, the wealth enrichment of your house is about how you maximise your wealth through exploiting opportunities, working hard and so on. The wealth area of your garden, on the other hand, is concerned with influencing how other people affect your wealth – whether your boss puts you forward for promotion, whether your numbers come up in the lottery, or whether your long-lost uncle writes you into his will.

So you have overlaid the Pah Kwa on to your garden just as you did with your house, and you have worked out where each of the enrichments falls. Now consider what you use the garden for, and see whether you are using the garden in harmony with its feng shui or in conflict with it.

Do you have a barbecue? Which area does it fall in? If it's in your wealth area you could be burning money. Much better to have it in your friends enrichment, or in pleasure and indulgence. Which area of the garden do your children play in? Where do you keep the lawnmower? If you use herbs for healing, are they in the health enrichment? Walk the Nine Palaces in your garden and think about everything you use it for, and then consider whether each one is sited as well as it could be.

THROUGH THE GARDEN GATE
≡

The entrance to your garden is crucial; you need to encourage the ch'i to come in, and to flow smoothly. As a general rule, whatever encourages ch'i will also encourage people, so stand back and take a good, long, objective look at your garden entrance. Does it make you want to come in?

You want an entrance through which the ch'i flows neither too fast nor too slow; you will need to consider which direction your garden faces and work to balance its influence. If the front garden faces south you have a yang garden with nourishing ch'i from the south coming

133

towards it. This is strong, fresh, open ch'i, so the potential risk is that it will flow too fast and become accelerated. So you may need to slow the ch'i down and encourage it to bend and curve. If there is no boundary to your garden you should erect one – a low hedge or a trellis will still give an open feel to the garden.

Make the ch'i find its way through the gate more gently by putting an arch over the gate, but don't let it lead into a tunnel of arches or the ch'i will become arrowed. Tone down the bright, yang feel of the garden, if necessary, by making sure there is some dappled shade from a fruit tree or some other tree that is not too dark and dominant.

The aim is not to cancel out the yang feel of the garden, but to tone it down so that it doesn't become overpowering.

If, on the other hand, your front garden faces north, you will want to introduce as many yang elements as possible to what should be a yang area, otherwise the northerly, yin features will dominate your fame enrichment which should be open, welcoming and public. So with a north-facing front garden you should open it up, remove or at least reduce boundaries, especially on the south side, and create more light in the garden by pruning or removing large, dark trees and shrubs. And as far as the entrance is concerned just have a low gate, or an open-work lattice or wrought iron one.

Don't forget to consider the ground surface. Is it paved, grassed or gravelled? If it is covered in a dark surface, perhaps you could resurface it with a light-coloured gravel, for instance? This would help to lighten up the whole front aspect of the house.

Consider which way your garden faces, and create an entrance that suits it. Low and open entrances will encourage ch'i from the direction the garden faces, more solid gates or archways will slow the ch'i down as it enters the garden.

DRIVEWAYS AND ENTRANCE PATHS

Ch'i will flow along the driveway, or the path to the front door if you park on the road, so you don't want it to be too long and straight or it will funnel the ch'i. If it is narrower towards the house this will create even more of a funnel effect, although if it opens out too far as it reaches the house the ch'i will be weakened. The ideal driveway or entrance path sweeps in a wide, gentle curve, and slopes slightly away from the house. However, you don't want it to slope steeply or money and good luck will roll away down it. If it slopes steeply down to the house it will carry the ch'i too fast.

A semi-circular driveway is wonderful if you're lucky enough to have room for one, since it allows the ch'i to flow towards and away from the house in the sweeping curve in which ch'i likes to move.

BOUNDARIES

If you want to encourage ch'i from a particular direction, keep the boundary on that side of the garden low, or at least open. If you don't want to reduce the height of the boundary use a hedge that isn't too dense – such as beech – or erect a trellis. These are much more open than solid fences or walls and still allow the ch'i through.

While you may need to reduce the boundary height or density to let the ch'i through, it isn't a good idea to remove the boundary altogether. If you don't mark the boundary between your garden and your neighbours' in some way, you will share the ch'i flowing around their garden, which may not carry with it the peaceful and harmonious energy that you want to encourage. You have no control over the ch'i on their side of the boundary, and you don't know what goes on in their house or garden that may influence it. So make sure you have a boundary that encourages or slows down the ch'i to suit you.

If you want to inhibit the ch'i from a particular direction, simply make the boundary more solid. Suppose you find that money always slips through your hands because you spend it all on going out, entertaining and socialising. Try opening up the boundary in your wealth enrichment, and filling it in or raising the height along the boundary of your pleasure and indulgence enrichment.

CHANGING LEVELS

Remember the ideal landscape in which to site a house? You want the green hills of the Green Dragon to the east, where the sun rises. South of the house, the area of the Red Phoenix, the land should slope away gently. In the west should be the flat plains of the White Tiger, preferably with a stream blocking his unpredictable ch'i. And in the north the Black Tortoise should nurture you with hills to protect you.

Few people are lucky enough to live in a perfect landscape, but you can recreate this landscape in miniature if you want to, at least in the areas where you need it most. If you already have buildings taller than your house to the north these will already fulfil the role of the hills of the black tortoise, for example. But if the area to the east slopes away from the house, why not create the hills of the dragon in your garden? Of course, I'm not suggesting that you create a mountain in your back garden, but you could raise the level along the boundary with a rockery or a raised flower bed, or even a greenhouse.

To the south you could make sure that your own garden slopes away from the house, even if you can't control what happens to the lie of the land outside your boundary. And in the west, you could create a stream or pond to protect you from the more dangerous effects of the White Tiger's influence.

PAVED AREAS

There are three main points to consider when it comes to paved areas:

 the material you use
 the overall shape
 the layout of the slabs or bricks.

Materials

As far as the material you use is concerned, consider whether it makes that part of your garden darker, lighter or more colourful. Do you need to lighten up a dark area, tone down too much glaring light in the south if the ch'i has degenerated into accelerating sha, or introduce colour to liven up stagnating ch'i from the north-east?

Shape

The next consideration is the overall shape. This should be regular – the Chinese would never use an abstract-shaped area, so you should go for a circle, semi-circle, square, octagon or something of the sort. Circles or octagons are preferable as a rule, unless you need to introduce a straight-line remedy to the area.

Layout of paving

The layout of paving is important as well. Use a regular pattern, but one which avoids too many straight lines. Large areas of paving may need breaking up, either with pots and tubs of plants, or even with plants grown between the paving. Scented plants are especially good, since beautiful scents encourage ch'i and discourage sha – you could try thyme, camomile or dianthus.

137

PATHS

The straighter the path, the more it will encourage ch'i to flow down it and the faster that ch'i will flow. Is this what you want? If the path runs from the south it will bring vigorous yang ch'i with it. If the area it flows into is dark and sleepy, you want the ch'i to enliven it and a straight path will encourage this. But if the area is already too yang – too open and public – you will want to moderate this ch'i with a path that bends and curves. For example, suppose your back garden faces south; you want to maintain a nurturing yin feel to it, so although you don't want to block out the vigorous ch'i from the south you do want to calm it down a little.

Any paths leading into the garden from the west should undulate and curve in order to pacify any dangerous sha coming from the direction of the White Tiger.

BEDS AND BORDERS

Flower beds and borders should follow much the same principle as paths: where you want to encourage the ch'i, or where you need a straight line remedy in the south-west or in your health enrichment, use beds with straight edges. But where you want to calm down the flow of ch'i, use curving edges.

If you have a border with a straight back to it such as a wall or hedge, you can create flowing curves along the front edge. These should be broad, sweeping curves that don't need to be regular in shape. But island flower beds set into a lawn or an area of paving or gravel should be a regular shape. If you need straight lines use a square or rectangular shape; if you need curves use a circular or oval-shaped flower bed. If you are adding a flower bed to an area where the feng shui is already nicely in balance and you don't want to upset the harmony of it, use either a circular bed or an octagonal one.

STATUES AND ORNAMENTS

Statues and ornaments are extremely useful in a garden where you need to introduce a remedy. Any coloured object can be used where a colour remedy is required, especially in the north-east and in the children enrichment – for example, a coloured, ceramic bird bath so the children can watch and learn about birds.

Statues are also especially useful where you need a stillness remedy. Stillness remedies are best in the west or in your pleasure enrichment – where better to place something beautiful to look at? You can also use some statues and ornaments where you need a straight-line remedy (south-west, or in your health enrichment). Some abstract pieces of modern sculpture are particularly suitable for this.

GARDEN SEATS

You need to consider which of the enrichments you want to put a seat in. It would be ideal in your pleasure area, but a seat in your fame area? Do you really want to sit back and rest on your laurels? A seat in your relationship area would be excellent if your relationship needs time for relaxation and nurturing. But some relationships need positive action to preserve them, for example if you spend long periods apart and both have to work hard to keep the relationship flourishing. If this is the case, it may not be a good idea to sit back for too long. So think about which enrichment you want to put your garden seat in.

Having said that, it is certainly a good idea for every garden to have somewhere in it where you can sit and relax – just make sure you pick the right spot. When it comes to choosing the seat itself, think about the shape of it, and any pattern that it incorporates. A bench seat with a slatted seat and back is made up of straight lines that will encourage ch'i. However, a wrought iron chair with a round seat and round back decorated with a pattern made up of curving flower shapes will help to slow down ch'i that is travelling too fast.

WATER IN THE GARDEN

The Chinese consider water essential to a garden. It may be only a bird bath or a small pond, although they would always choose moving water if possible – a stream or fountain, for example. Ch'i loves water, which encourages it into an area and then helps it to circulate smoothly and harmoniously. Water also encourages wildlife, and bringing life into the garden can only improve its feng shui.

If you have young children, there are still water features that are safe to use. You can have a little water bubbling up through an arrangement of cobbles, or a fountain spilling from a wall on to paving below and flowing down through the cracks so there is no standing water anywhere. Electric pumps and other equipment for creating water features are very easy and inexpensive to buy in garden centres.

If you decide to create a pond – or better still, a series of two or more ponds that empty into one another – use natural materials such as stone or wood for any visible parts of the construction; Ch'i doesn't care for impervious, artificial substances such as plastic or fibreglass. Build a raised edge around your pond to sit on, and if it is in your wealth enrichment, keep goldfish in it.

Water is the one feature that can be adapted to provide any one of the eight remedies. It can be used as a light remedy, if the surface of it reflects the light into dark areas that need lifting. It is also a sound remedy if the water can be heard moving, for example if you have a fountain. A fountainhead, a ceramic bird bath or a pool with a mosaic bottom to it are all examples of how your water feature can bring colour to your garden. If you need a life remedy, put goldfish in the pool – this is also a movement remedy, as is a fountain or stream. A cool, smooth pool, however small, brings stillness, and if you need a straight-line remedy, create a straight-sided channel to bring the water from its source into a pond. And if you need a mechanical device, what could be better than a fountain?

TREES AND PLANTS

Anything living creates good feng shui in the garden, and that includes plants as well as animals. The important thing to consider with any kind of plant, from the tallest tree to the smallest flower, is the shape of it. First of all, think about the overall shape: is it tall and straight like a conifer or a bamboo, or is it rounded and curvy like a maple or a peony? In general, you should use the more rounded shapes, unless you need straight lines to move the ch'i along faster.

The next thing to consider is the shape of the leaves. Again, go for more rounded shapes like apple trees or nasturtiums, rather than thin, pointed leaves like pine needles or chives, unless there is a reason to go for the sharper shapes. You should also avoid plants with thorns unless they have a good scent, or a very rounded shape or leaves to counteract the sharpness of the thorns.

There are certain things that will always bring good feng shui with them. One of them is sweet scents, so you can include any plant that smells beautiful regardless of its shape. Good examples of this include roses, lilies and lavender. Old age is always venerated by the Chinese, so show respect for any mature trees in your garden – even if they are tall and sharp-leaved – since their experience and accumulated wisdom can only bring good to you. Such trees have very powerful ch'i of their own and you shouldn't interfere with it.

Climbing plants are particularly useful since they will break up a bare expanse of wall and give softness to the hard corners of the house. Scented climbers are the best of all, such as roses, honeysuckle, scented clematis and wisteria.

TRULY TINY GARDENS

Even if your garden is tiny, you can still improve its feng shui. Ch'i hates untidiness, clutter and dirt. So if you have a small backyard, get out there and clear the junk, clean it up and tidy the dustbins – better still, screen them off or move them somewhere else. There now – you've already improved the feng shui.

The next thing to do is to break up any hard edges, and soften the look of the place. If you have a hard, depressing ground surface, try something softer such as gravel, or a herringbone arrangement of soft-coloured, weathered brick. Or you could grow plants between cracks in the paving stones – just throw around a few packets of seeds such as love-in-a-mist or opium poppies which will grow almost anywhere. Look at your back gate. Is there anything you can do to improve it? Could you paint it, or even replace it, or put an arch over it?

Now introduce a little life to the place with a few plants. Just one or two pots with climbers to break up the flatness of the walls, and a pot or two of flowers with at least one or two evergreens to see you through the winter, are better than nothing. If you're short of space, even a hanging basket by the door is far better than nothing. The round shape of hanging baskets is excellent for encouraging ch'i to flow harmoniously.

There are other things you can try as well. You can add colour by painting the walls or fences, or covering them with a painted trellis. And how about a statue or an ornament? Even a gnarled piece of driftwood or a beautiful stone you have collected will help the feng shui. Have you got room for a little pond, or even a small fountain? Wind chimes will create a pleasant sound when you step out of your back door. And maybe somewhere to sit out, now you've created somewhere worth sitting?

You can always create something that will encourage ch'i to enter your garden. Even if you only have a window box or a hanging basket you can make sure it is always tidy, there are no dead plants in it, and it is healthy and full of life and colour. If you have a window box you might also want to think about the shape of it: it is better to have a window box with a curved front edge than a straight one. And it should be made of a natural material – wood or terracotta are better than plastic.

So you see, even the tiniest garden of all can still help to bring you good feng shui, if you just put a little bit of thought into it. And before you know it, you could find yourself hanging baskets and window boxes from every window in your house. Then you'll have a garden that can bring you as much good fortune as anyone else's.

7

FENG SHUI
IN BUSINESS

One sees great things from the valley;
Only small things from the peak.

CHESTERTON

All the basic principles of feng shui are the same in business as they are at home, of course. But there are several additional things you need to know to create the most harmonious work space possible, which will maximise your success and your earning potential.

WHERE TO SITE YOUR BUSINESS

If you run your own business, or are about to start one up, the first thing to consider is where to locate it. The first thing you should do when you find a possible office, shop or factory site, is to find out something about its previous occupants. Have they all thrived? Or gone bankrupt? This will tell you more about its feng shui than anything – it is hard evidence of the good or bad influences on the property.

You need to look at the place in the context of its surroundings, so finding out about the success or otherwise of neighbouring businesses is also an important clue. Are they doing good business? Do their premises look pleasant and inviting to potential customers? This may sound like plain common sense to you, and nothing to do with feng shui. But feng shui is all about common sense – ch'i knows what it's doing, and it naturally chooses to flow where it feels welcome and not where it doesn't.

The next thing to think about is the entrance. Is it as welcoming as it could be? Is the door the right size in proportion to the building? The rules that apply here are the same as those that we have already looked at in Chapter 5.

ROADS AND BUSINESS

When the art of feng shui was first developed, rivers and streams were all important (hence 'wind and water', the literal meaning of 'feng shui'), since water helps to carry ch'i in a flowing and harmonious way. Raging torrents were not considered good, since these channelled the ch'i too fast and aggressively; water should meander and eddy gently. A river should not flow straight towards the house and then veer off at the last minute – it should run past it in gentle curves.

All these principles still apply to rivers and streams, but for most of us, the modern-day equivalent of a river is a road. So these rules apply to roads as well. They shouldn't funnel the ch'i too straight at the building, and roads with curves are better than fast, straight roads.

If you are buying or renting property, you can make sure you choose a location with a road running past the front door, and preferably on a corner. But what if you are already ensconced in a building? If it faces a junction with a road pointing directly towards it, hang a mirror on the door to deflect the ch'i. If it is a glass door, with a wall beyond it that faces the road, you can hang a mirror on this wall instead, if you prefer. If two or more roads are pointing at the building in an arrow shape, this is even more threatening; again, hang a mirror to deflect it.

145

YOUR OFFICE GROUND PLAN
≡

Now overlay the Pah Kwa on to a ground plan of your office. This should tell you where to locate the various functions. Keep your money – or your till – in the wealth enrichment. If you put it in the pleasure area you may be tempted to spend all your profits. Put the staff room in the family enrichment to encourage good relations. And your reception area should be in the fame enrichment, of course.

Go round the Pah Kwa and see where each enrichment falls, and then allocate the rooms and offices to the most suitable area. If you have no reception area – if customers don't visit the premises – or if it cannot be in the fame enrichment, you could use the fame area for your marketing department instead.

Remember how ch'i likes to flow. It won't be happy if your offices consist of dark corridors with lots of closed doors leading off them. Go for a more open-plan arrangement, with screens and plants to break it up.

If any of the offices are small and cramped, and you cannot open up the layout, use mirrors to enlarge the feel of the room; you could put mirrors all along one or two of the walls. This is especially useful if it helps to reflect a pleasant view from the window.

Make sure that the doors in the building open into the rooms, and not on to walls. If necessary, re-hang the doors to free-up the ch'i. Failing this, use a mirror on the wall so that as you enter through the door it reflects a view of the room.

As with feng shui at home, any corners jutting into rooms should be softened with plants, and any alcoves and corners should be brought into the room with bright lighting, plants, or mechanical devices which mean that the corner is used regularly. And large, blank wall spaces should be broken up with pictures, or at least the occasional wall planner.

USING FENG SHUI TO RESOLVE EMPLOYEE PROBLEMS

If you have problems with a particular employee, look at the feng shui of his or her work area and see if you can improve it. Here are a few examples:

- ☻ An employee who is frequently off sick – move the office or desk into the health enrichment. At the very least, draw up a plan of the employee's office and move the desk to the health enrichment within the room.
- ☻ An employee who is prone to leave early should sit in a place where the outside door can't be seen.
- ☻ An employee who is difficult to get on with – make sure the employee's office isn't at the end of a corridor with sharp bends in it. Or perhaps it has a door that is always closed, or opens on to a wall. If the ch'i finds it difficult to reach this person, so will your staff.
- ☻ An employee who spends too much time socialising – check to see whether the office or desk is in an unsuitable enrichment of the building or of the room. The most obvious one to avoid is the pleasure enrichment – move them to the wealth or wisdom area.
- ☻ An employee who is depressed – this will affect the employee's work, so it is in everyone's interests to improve things. There may be influences outside work that affect that person's mood, but you can still help. Put the desk somewhere that the ch'i flows smoothly round an open, spacious bright area, in the pleasure enrichment of the building or at least of the room.

THE POSITION OF YOUR DESK

If you work for someone else you may have been feeling that this chapter has nothing to do with you (unless you can convert your boss to recognise the benefits of good feng shui). But most of us have some control over whereabouts in the office our desk is sited. And just about all of us control the arrangement of our own desktop, which we'll come to in a minute.

So where should the desk be? First of all, as you probably realise by now, you should be able to see the door when you're sitting at the desk. This means that you are in a 'superior attitude' as the Chinese call it. You may even be one of those sensitive people who has always felt uncomfortable with your back to a door, in which case you will understand this principle instinctively. This means you should never sit facing a wall. If you really cannot avoid this – perhaps your boss won't let you change it – hang a mirror on the wall in front of you to act as a rear-view mirror.

It is also inadvisable to sit with your back to a window, since this makes you unaware of the ch'i entering the room from this direction. If you can't avoid this, place a mirror so that you can see the window reflected in it. It is especially bad to sit with your back to an interior window, since this is an ambivalent design feature – an outdoor feature inside the building. If you can't move the desk, either remove the partition or block the window creating another wall. You can do this by painting it out, obscuring with a screen or hanging a blind that you always keep down.

It is not a good idea to set the desk across the corner of the room at an angle, either, since this creates a dead corner behind you. However, it is all right so long as you create some life or activity in this corner with a pot plant, perhaps, or a mechanical device such as a printer or fax machine.

It is also a bad idea to have a desk 'floating' in the middle of the room with space all round it, since the ch'i flows too freely around it and onward, taking the fruits of your hard work with it.

So what's left? The ideal position for the desk is where one of its short sides is against the wall, to give it some kind of anchor point, and you can clearly see anyone coming in through the door. If your back is against a wall in this position, make sure the desk is far enough away from it that you can move freely. If you are cramped getting in and out of your chair, the ch'i will also be cramped reaching you, which means that your energy for work, and your achievements, will be restricted.

SHARING OFFICES

Perhaps you share an office with someone else? In this case, you need to make sure that both of you are in a good position, in view of the door. You could place your desks diagonally across neighbouring corners, so long as you both use the corners behind you to stop them becoming dead areas. Or one of you could set the short side of your desk against the back of the other desk instead of against a wall; this will create a T-shape or an L-shape.

It's not a good idea to sit directly facing each other with no space between the desks, unless there is a partial screen between the two of you (such as computer screens). This is especially true if one of you is senior to the other.

If a boss and an assistant share an office, the one with the most 'superior position' will dominate – in other words, the one who is facing the door with the desk furthest away from it. If this is your situation and you are the boss, make sure you have the best desk position. (Perhaps you may want to arrange this even if you're not the boss.)

If several people share an office, make sure the desks are not laid out in neat rows – as in a traditional typing pool – since this will funnel the ch'i along channels between the desks. Arrange them more randomly and create a classic, open-plan layout, broken up with screens to help the ch'i wander freely in and out around the room.

THE FENG SHUI OF YOUR DESK

You can overlay the Pah Kwa on to a plan of your desk, and see whether you have arranged it in the best possible way. For a start it should be neat and tidy, since ch'i hates clutter. You may not find this easy, but at least tidy it at the beginning or end of each day, even if you can't keep it neat in between.

Now overlay the Pah Kwa; the section of the desk where you sit is the fame enrichment. Facing you is the relationship area – this is the place to keep a photograph of your loved ones. At the right-hand end of the desk is your wisdom enrichment – keep your reference books or important files here, or your computer. At the left-hand end is the pleasure enrichment – a good place for your tea or coffee mug. The friends enrichment is in the top left-hand corner so this is the ideal place for the telephone. In the top right-hand corner is your children enrichment, the place to keep files or floppy disks containing all the information about your new projects – your children. The bottom left-hand corner is the health area; perhaps you use an ioniser or an air freshener? If so, this is the place to keep it. And the bottom right-hand corner is the wealth area – where better to keep the petty cash?

This is not a definitive desk layout – you may not have a computer. Or you might want to keep new project files in the enrichment of friends and new beginnings in the top left-hand corner of the desk, or photographs in your children enrichment. It's just an indication of how you can maximise the positive ch'i flowing around your desk by thinking about the arrangement of your desktop from the point of view of its feng shui.

ELECTRICAL EQUIPMENT IN OFFICES

Almost all offices nowadays are full of computers, faxes, photocopiers and other electrical equipment. These are all mechanical devices which stir up and enliven ch'i. There are places – as you have learnt by now – where this is a very good thing. But be aware that you can have too much of it, which will create stress and excess nervous energy which can lead to arguments and conflict. If this happens, try to move some of the equipment into another area of the office. And introduce some stillness remedies to counteract the effect, such as a large, heavy filing cabinet, or a decorative statue.

8

TROUBLESHOOTING
WITH FENG SHUI

*Wash what is dirty, water what is dry, heal what
   is wounded.*
*Bend what is stiff, warm what is cold, guide what
   goes off the road.*

ARCHBISHOP STEPHEN LANGTON, 1228 CE

PART I ENRICHMENT PROBLEMS

Here are some easy-to-carry-out tips if you are experiencing
problems connected with any of the eight enrichments.
These things should be done before you attempt to
implement any remedies. Always have a ten-point plan to
regularly mentally check your house or office. This plan
should include the following and they are in no particular
order of importance – although if one was more important
than the others then I would suggest that it is the first.

- clutter
- life
- windows
- heating
- lighting/mirrors
- drainage
- doors
- electrics
- colour
- paths

Let's look at each of these in turn, and remember the following are tips and suggestions – nothing with feng shui is set in stone. You may find that some of these don't apply, or you have different ideas about them – that's fine. Do whatever you have to do to make your life flow smoothly, successfully and satisfyingly. If you experience problems then you need to make changes. If everything is going well then maybe it's best to leave well alone – if it ain't broke, don't fix it.

CLUTTER

We all collect clutter – there's no avoiding the stuff. It materialises around us like dust under the sofa. Whatever we do, clutter will sneak into our lives and homes. The only thing you can do is be very strict about yourself – and clear clutter out from time to time. Ever looked in your kitchen drawers? And I mean really looked. What have you got there? Old plastic carrier bags? Bits of string you've saved and know full well you're never going to use? Whatever it is, throw it away – chances are you're not going to use them.

Check cupboards, especially the one under the stairs. And while you're at it, go and check the garage. The garage is a bit like our subconscious – we can't see it so assume it's fine. Well, its probably not. This is the place we collect all the junk that tells us about how our life has been in the past – pots of old, half-used paint; rolls of carpet we'll never need; broken tools and machinery that will never get fixed and have probably been replaced by now with ones that do work; toys left over from when the children were young and we can't bear to throw away. You name it, it'll be there. It's clutter. There's nothing for it but to throw it all away if you want the ch'i to flow smoothly and well around and through your home. And how long since you checked the attic? Under the bed?

Old suitcases on top of the wardrobe? Boxes of old clothes

and shoes on the landing? Chest of drawers full of last year's clothes. No, we're not being fashion conscious here, merely clutter-less. If clothes don't fit, are worn out, need repairing, look dreadful, have gone out of fashion, no longer suit you, whatever, there really is no alternative – throw them away. Or better still pack them into a big bag and take them down to your local charity shop. Boy George, the pop singer, did this recently and admits to sending 40 bags of clothing, in a single year, to the charity Oxfam. How many could you send?

Don't ignore the emotional clutter as well. Clear out your head from time to time. Throw away all those old love letters, photographs of old loves who you can't even remember any more, anything that reminds you of anyone you have had problems with or carry any resentment towards.

In the office you can strip out your files from time to time. If you haven't looked at a piece of paper for three months or more chances are you'll never look at it again. Obviously, in an office there are various official documents that you can't throw away for legal reasons such as the Inland Revenue requirements – well, store it somewhere else. Perhaps down in the basement?

Throw away old magazines, newspapers, envelopes and brochures. Every now and again pull out units in the kitchen, if it's physically possible, and clean behind them. You'd be surprised how much clutter collects behind a washing machine or fridge.

Make sure no dust collects under your bed. Carpets should be vacuumed regularly and rugs taken into the garden and beaten from time to time. Check what you're keeping on your book shelves as well. We all have an amazing tendency to keep and collect books that will never be read again – and yet we just can't bear to throw them away. Find somewhere to store them and allow the ch'i to circulate freely.

Check what lurks above shelves and cupboards as well. If cobwebs can collect dust and dead flies then they can collect ch'i. If a spider has finished with a web and moved on to a new one, what are you saving the old one for?

*L*IFE

You are life – you are the *jen* in the centre of your home. But is that enough? Feng shui suggests that to be in tune with nature we need to bring nature inside with us – to remind us of something bigger going on in our lives than just getting up and going to work. Fill your home with plants – pot plants, house plants, bonsai trees, climbers, vines, ivy, herbs on window sills, whatever takes your fancy. Plants in pots are easy to maintain, easy to replace if they start looking a bit tatty, easy to look after if we go away a lot (you just need a friend and some water), easy for colour, life, interest and friendliness. A home without life is too stark and sterile.

Cut flowers are frowned on in feng shui as they are full of dying ch'i leaking away – and it leaks into your home. If you simply must have cut flowers change the water every day – and throw them away when they're dead. Also any dead pot plants must be thrown away and replaced immediately. Dried flowers are not suitable, either.

Watch the pots you put your plants in – they should be made of natural materials – terracotta or stoneware. Avoid plastic if you can. The colours of the pots should be checked to make sure they harmonise with the rest of the colour scheme – it's all too easy to just not notice a simple pot and yet it can throw the decor completely.

Plants with long, pointed leaves aren't recommended – it's better to have round leaves that look like money. Dead-head any flowers as soon as they have finished.

And don't forget that it isn't only plants that can bring life into a home – how about a cat? Or a dog? Or mice, hamsters, birds, lizards, even stick insects? A cat curled up on a cushion is a good way of introducing life into an area that needs remedying. Of course, the trick is getting the cat to stay still.

And don't forget the best of all feng shui remedies – fish. Make sure you always have an odd number and keep the aquarium in your wealth enrichment to promote money and income.

Windows

You want a simple tip? Keep them clean. That's it. Clean windows allow the ch'i to enter and leave freely. Keep the curtains pulled well back from the windows to allow maximum light to enter and make sure you don't have any windows un-curtained at night. For feng shui purposes an exposed window looking out on to the black night is considered a very bad omen.

If you want blinds at your windows they should be made of natural materials, if possible – wood is good, as is cotton fabric. Try to avoid plastics if you can. Watch the colours of blinds, as the ch'i filters through it will take on the resonance of the blind colour. This may be good if you want that colour quality in a particular room.

Curtains that hang down limply either side of a window aren't considered very good feng shui. They should have a little swag or curve to them. And ideally they should reach to the floor. When they're drawn back they should be tied either side so they hang in graceful folds. And allow more material for your curtains than you think you need. Too much is preferable to too little. When the curtains are drawn together at night there should be masses of fabric hanging in pleats and folds rather than something that looks as if it just meets in the middle.

Curtains should match the seasons as well – heavy drapes for the winter and lighter, finer fabrics for the summer. It's good to take your curtains down twice a year and clean them, anyway.

Curtains should be capable of being drawn and opened easily – if you've got to tug hard on them then there's something blocking the flow of ch'i. Watch the track that they move on. Again, you're looking for natural materials. A wooden pole with rings is good – bamboo even better. Plastic tracking is not really good.

Windows should be capable of being opened if that's what they were intended to do. Any that are stuck with paint should be freed. Keep windows well painted – this isn't only feng shui, it's home maintenance – they last longer if they're painted. Check the colours of any woodwork on windows on the outside of the house and make sure it harmonises with the rest of the house.

Heating

When you've finished with your wood-burning stove or open fire for the winter then clear out the ashes and throw them away, and have the chimney swept now rather than at the last minute just before you light the fire for the first time in the autumn.

If you have central heating be aware that the sound of water in radiators, pumps, boilers firing up and the creak of metal as radiators and pipes cool down or heat up all bring sound into your home – and it may affect any sound remedies you're working with.

Radiators should be as discreet as possible. If you can hide them, so much the better.

In an ideal home there would always be an open fire. If, because of local regulations, you can't have one then maybe you can get away with an imitation one – but it must be realistic. Those old-fashioned fires which relied on a single light bulb with a bit of coloured plastic aren't really suitable at all.

157

Electric wall heaters that blow hot air do really weird things to the ch'i in a room and they should be used only if there is no other solution. A convector heater may be better. Be aware that lights, computers, candles, stereos, ovens, cookers, any electrical equipment, all generate heat – and as heat rises so does the ch'i. A very slow-moving ceiling fan can help to push the ch'i back down into the room and it stops you feeling too drained. Ceiling fans are also very good movement remedies.

Any heating and ventilation ducts should be cleaned regularly, and extractor fans serviced at the right time.

*L*IGHTING/MIRRORS

One simple tip – if you can see bare light bulbs that's bad feng shui. All lighting should be discreet. Any harsh glares should be eliminated. Avoid shades that let you see down inside them – and hence see the bulb. Lights should do just that – light up things to enable you to see better – but they shouldn't be obvious. White light can be a strain on the eyes. Daylight bulbs are better. Lamps should throw gentle pools of light rather than harshly illuminate. Overhead lights, ideally, should be on dimmer switches so you can regulate how much light they give out.

You don't have to restrict yourself to electric lights. Candles can give out just as much light – and it's softer and much more gentle on the eyes, and more natural. Oil lamps give a very soft glow. And firelight is so soothing.

Mirrors are for reflecting and looking into. How can we do this if they are misted up, dirty, aged and cracked? Keep mirrors clean and bright. Mirrors, if they're the sort you look into rather than remedies, should be at head height. That may sound obvious, but so many people have mirrors that are too low or too high. But what about little people, I hear you ask, how can they look into my mirrors? Simple. Angle them so they lean slightly away from the wall at the top and then everybody can see themselves clearly in them.

Mirrors used as remedies should be small and discreet. If you can get hold of the octagonal Pah Kwa mirrors which have the eight trigrams on them so much the better. To deflect sha, mirrors should be placed so they face outwards. To channel ch'i inside the house, you'll have to angle them so they do their job properly.

One tip you might like to try is to have a large mirror angled on a wall so it reflects a beautiful view into the room when you're sitting in your favourite chair, or lying in bed, or relaxing in the bath.

Avoid mirrors that have pictures engraved or printed on them. Bad taste is also bad feng shui. Oval mirrors are good – especially if they have ornate wooden surrounds. Mirrors should be the highest quality you can afford. And they make good remedies for when you need to see behind you. If you have to have your back to the door in an office or the kitchen you can position a mirror so that you can always see if there is someone behind you – a very important aspect of feng shui.

DRAINAGE

The drains are the digestive system of your house. If they are blocked, the waste ch'i can't be eliminated – and it will fester, as will any water trapped in blocked pipes.

Clear out the gutters and get rid of the winter's leaves that invariably collect there. Make sure your garden drains well – pools of muddy water lying on the lawn aren't helpful.

Check that all taps can be turned off completely and that nothing leaks or drips. Lavatories should be kept with both the seat and lid down. Sinks and baths should be disinfected regularly, and all stains and marks removed from enamel surfaces. Any chrome work on taps and shower attachments should be kept brightly sparkling.

Any outside drainage systems should be regularly inspected for blockages, and if any are found they should be cleared at once. Inspection covers to drains should be firmly in place, and any that are cracked or broken should be replaced.

Any sinks or baths that are chipped, cracked, or broken in any way should be replaced. Make sure the area under sinks, such as in kitchens, is kept clear of clutter, and clean.

Any cold-water storage tanks in attics or roof spaces should be inspected and covered if open. Hot water systems should be checked for leaks, rusting or blockages.

Any washing-up equipment that is past its best should be replaced: this includes scourers, cloths, wire brushes, pan cleaners and cleaning fluids. Washing-up bowls should be replaced regularly and, ideally, there should be at least two – one for plates and one for food items.

If you have a pond in the garden this should be drained and cleaned every now and again to avoid stagnant water, mud and the build-up of too much weed.

DOORS

Oil hinges and locks regularly to avoid doors sticking. Make sure they open silently so eliminate any squeaks or rattles. Doors should be kept well painted – especially any external doors – and avoid over-harsh gloss paints: a matt, satin or silk finish is best. This avoids too much reflection which turns the door into a giant mirror – maybe in the place where you didn't want a mirror remedy.

Keep doors for the purpose for which they are intended – which isn't as hat stands, coat racks or the storage of your dressing gown. Doors are for opening and allowing fresh ch'i to enter, and for closing to stop ch'i leaving. If you have a space where there used to be a door and it isn't there any longer, but the surround is, then try to replace the door. If you have a door that isn't used any more it is probably best to remove it and partition the area off properly.

Stable doors can be beneficial in that you can open the top half to let in air in the summer much like a window. But make sure that neither half sticks; they should be able to be opened smoothly and effortlessly.

Doors are like the nervous system of a house – if they stick they will irritate and cause tension. They allow communication to happen so they should be able to be freely opened and closed, and easy to pass through. Double doors which open in the middle should have both halves opened at the same time rather than trying to squeeze through one half that is too small.

Any door fittings in the way of handles, knockers, letter boxes and bolts should be kept polished and clean. Outside doors should be painted in sympathy with the rest of the house.

*E*LECTRICS

If ch'i likes to follow curving lines what could be more attractive than electric cables – and what could be worse? Go round your house and see how many electric cables you have snaking behind desks, down bedside tables, across work surfaces, across floors – and they all head in the same direction – downwards. And that's where the ch'i ends up – on the floor. If you can hide the cables so much the better, but I do realise how difficult that can be. You can at least bundle them up and pin them along the edge of the floor or tape them to the back of a cupboard.

Check the safety of all electrical equipment. Electric pollution is present in most homes and it affects our nerves and can make us feel tense and irritable.

Don't forget all those telephone wires coiling across the floor. And, of course, check how the electricity cables come into your home.

Check fuse boxes are in working order and make sure they are discreet and hidden away, and that there are no loose or broken wires there.

We all live inside powerful 'ring mains' which act as giant magnets and the effects on our health may be detrimental – and yet how many of us could live without such power, such energy, now? If we have to live with it we can at least make it our servant instead of the other way round. As we get more technology we get more electric pollution around us and maybe we can occasionally stop and take stock of what we are accumulating. Electrical appliances are powerful mechanical object remedies. When feng shui was first devised there were no electrical gadgets so there was no need to take them into account. Now, however, they have taken the first place as a remedy in our home – and as such have become a curse rather than a cure. The secret is to try to eliminate them – or at least try to contain them into some order or put them into areas where they will do the least harm.

Living near, or under, pylons has been proved to be disastrous health-wise and I can only advise you to move.

COLOUR

Feng shui is not interior decoration – and I'm not about to tell you what colours you should use to decorate your home. However, there are some tips that may prove useful. Use colours that are suitable to your element and compass direction (based on which astrological animal you are – see Appendix III).

- **Fire** – reds
- **Metal** – white and silver
- **Water** – blues
- **Wood** – greens
- **Earth** – yellow and browns
- **South** – strong reds

- ☺ **South-east** – reds, terracotta and yellows
- ☺ **East** – strong greens
- ☺ **North-east** – soft greens
- ☺ **North** – blues and black
- ☺ **North-west** – off-white shades
- ☺ **West** – white, with gold highlights
- ☺ **South-west** – browns, yellows or natural shades.

These colours also depend on which direction your house faces. Suppose you have a north-east facing house and you're the element metal – then you could combine soft greens with white and silver. Or if you have a south-facing house and you're the element earth you could use combinations of reds, oranges, yellows and browns – terracotta would be a good colour for you.

You can vary the colour of each enrichment depending on which compass direction it faces.

In an ideal house you would probably avoid patterned fabrics and wallpapers as they play havoc with ch'i. Use instead plain colours and simple colour schemes. Colour can become cluttered very easily. If you want your walls to have texture try using colour washes and sponging effects as they harmonise the ch'i rather than distracting it. It is also a very useful personal input – you form an intimate relationship with your house if you design, paint and decorate it yourself rather than buying something someone else designed.

If you were to stick to the four 'lucky' colours of red, white, black and gold that are so loved by the Chinese, you'd not go far wrong.

*P*ATHS

The path to your front door may be more important than you realise, in feng shui terms. It brings the world to you and brings you the dominant aspect of your personal ch'i.

Go outside and stand at the end of the path and look towards your house. What do you see? Be very critical, very objective. Now look out at the world. What do you see? How do the two marry up? Are they in harmony with each other? Is what you see pleasing? Harmonious? If not, why not? What will you do about it?

You need a clear path up to your front door, not too straight, and not too curved. The path shouldn't funnel or open out. Anything, like hedges or trees, that obscures the path should be removed, pruned, clipped or reshaped. If the path is obscured then so will both the ch'i and your personal 'face' – your reputation and fame.

PART II PERSONAL PROBLEMS

Each of the eight compass directions also relates to a particular person. So if you are experiencing problems with a certain person go to the enrichment or compass direction that 'belongs' to them and see if there's anything wrong there. If there is you can remedy it, change it, move something, alter the colour scheme or clear out the clutter and spring clean.

The eight 'people' are:

- *Ch'ien* – father – south
- *K'un* – mother – north
- *Chen* – eldest son – north-east
- *K'an* – middle son – west
- *Ken* – youngest son – north-west
- *H'sun* – eldest daughter – south-west
- *Li* – middle daughter – east
- *Tui* – youngest daughter – south-east.

These eight compass directions also refer to parts of our bodies. So again, if you are experiencing problems you can go to the relevant area and see what's wrong.

- 😊 *Ch'ien* – head and mind – south
- 😊 *K'un* – womb and belly – north
- 😊 *Chen* – feet – north-east
- 😊 *K'an* – ears – west
- 😊 *Ken* – hands – north-west
- 😊 *H'sun* – thighs and legs – south-west
- 😊 *Li* – eyes – east
- 😊 *Tui* – mouth – south-east.

And, of course, they refer to our emotions – so check your emotional state and check the compass direction.

- 😊 *Ch'ien* – creative energy – south
- 😊 *K'un* – nurturing love – north
- 😊 *Chen* – excitement, passion – north-east
- 😊 *K'an* – fear, apprehensions – west
- 😊 *Ken* – peace, tranquillity – north-west
- 😊 *H'sun* – compassion, kindness – south-west
- 😊 *Li* – dependency, receptiveness – east
- 😊 *Tui* – joy, satisfaction – south-east.

9

FENG SHUI AND
THE I CHING

At the western window I paused from writing;
The pines and bamboo were all buried in silence.
The moon rose and a calm wind came;
Suddenly, it was like an evening in the hills.
And so, as I dozed, I dreamed of the South West
And thought I was staying at the Hsien-Yu Palace.
When I woke and heard the dripping of the temple clock
I still thought it the trickle of the mountain stream.

WANG CHIEN, 756–835 CE

In the introduction we said that there were three distinct
types of feng shui – compass, directional and intuitive. Feng
shui and the *I Ching* fall into the third category. The *I Ching*
started out life as an almanac for farming and herbalists. It
was compiled – or devised – by Fu Hsi around 5,000 years
ago and may, according to some sources, be the most
ancient book on the planet. It influenced all of the Chinese
philosophers including Lao Tzu, the father of Taoism, and
Confucius who wrote a treatise, *The Ten Wings*, on it which
is still considered by scholars of the *I Ching* to be the most
indispensable source for anyone who wants an increased
insight into this most ancient of oracles.

USING THE *I CHING*
≡

Each of the compass directions has a trigram (see Chapter 2).
Your house or office faces in a particular direction as we saw

in Chapter 4. To work with the *I Ching* all you have to do is to combine the two to find which of the 64 hexagrams applies to each of your enrichments or rooms. For instance, the direction of south is a triple yang trigram, known as *Ch'ien*. If your house faces south then your fame enrichment would also be Ch'ien. Thus combined, you would have Ch'ien Ch'ien – or the very first hexagram, 1 – Chien – the Creative Power. The meaning of this is that you will be successful and you should continue in the direction you're going, but don't overdo things. You could then look up in a copy of the *I Ching* a full interpretation and, using your intuitive power, read what it says and feel how that applies to your enrichment or room. You may not need a full reading – sometimes just knowing the key word of the hexagram is enough to set you thinking.

Suppose your house faces north and you want to look up the enrichment Fa Chan – wealth. Well, this is facing north-west which gives you the trigram *Ken*, and the enrichment Fa Chan is *Tui*, which would give you the hexagram – 41 – Sun – Decreasing. The meaning of which is to watch what you're spending and economise – you may be called on to make sacrifices. That seems simple enough.

The trigram for the enrichment goes at the top and the trigram for the compass direction goes at the bottom to create the hexagram. As we have used the Early Heaven Sequence throughout the book we will continue with it here.

Overleaf is a chart for you to look up each of the 64 hexagrams and following that is a list of the 64 with a brief explanation of each of them. I have grouped them in eight groups – one for each of the eight compass directions to make it easier for you to see which 'belongs' to you.

Enrichment→ Compass direction ↓	Ch'ien Wang Ts'ai Fame	Chen T'ien Ch'ai Children	K'an Chang Yin Pleasure	Ken Chin Ts'ai Friends	K'un Chin Yin Rel/ship	H'sun An Lu Health	Li Fa Chan Wisdom	Tui Huan Lo Wealth
Ch'ien South	1	34	5	26	11	9	14	43
Chen North-east	25	51	3	27	24	42	21	17
K'an West	6	40	29	4	7	59	64	47
Ken North-west	33	62	39	52	15	53	56	31
K'un North	12	16	8	23	2	20	35	45
H'sun South-west	44	32	48	18	46	57	50	28
Li East	13	55	63	22	36	37	30	49
Tui South-east	10	54	60	41	19	61	38	58

South-facing house

- 😊 **Fame** – 1 – Ch'ien – the Creative Power – Success is yours – follow your path but don't overdo things.
- 😊 **Children** – 34 – Ta Chuang – Power of Greatness – Fortunate times – see things through – act wisely.
- 😊 **Pleasure** – 5 – Hsu – Waiting – Develop patience – others will help – relax.
- 😊 **Friends** – 26 – Ta Ch'u – Taming Force – Learn from past mistakes – success will come – you have great luck here.
- 😊 **Relationships** – 11 – T'ai – Calmness – Share with others your good fortune – be cautious – don't rush.
- 😊 **Health** – 9 – Hsiao Ch'u – Power of the Gentle – Be restrained – take things easy – clear away obstacles.
- 😊 **Wisdom** – 14 – Ta Yu – Great Possession – Work and study hard – success will come.
- 😊 **Wealth** – 43 – Kuai – Breakthrough – Be firm – you have to lose a little to gain a lot – you need assistance to win through – seek advice.

North-east-facing house

- 😊 **Fame** – 25 – Wu Wang – Correctness – Know your limits – all things change – things improve – be prepared.
- 😊 **Children** – 51 – Chen – Thunder – Stay calm – storms ahead – things pass – be resolute.
- 😊 **Pleasure** – 3 – Chun – Initial Difficulties – Enlist the co-operation of others – things start badly but finish well – be on your toes.
- 😊 **Friends** – 27 – I – Nourishment – Don't overdo it – gather strength – choose carefully.
- 😊 **Relationships** – 24 – Fu – Returning – Be patient – everything comes round again – you will find strength.
- 😊 **Health** – 42 – I Sun – Increasing – Everything is going well – plan ahead – luck is with you.
- 😊 **Wisdom** – 21 – Shih Ho – Cutting Through – You're on the right track – stay firm – keep your own counsel.

- **Wealth** – 17 – Sui – Following – Avoid arguments – put others in charge – be supple and bend.

West-facing house

- **Fame** – 6 – Sung – Conflict – Think carefully – act cautiously – stay calm.
- **Children** – 40 – Chieh – Removing Obstacles – Things go wrong – solve them, put them right – go back to how you were.
- **Pleasure** – 29 – K'an – Deep Well – Move ahead with great caution – there may be unforeseen problems – tread lightly.
- **Friends** – 4 – Meng – Inexperience – Learn from older people – gain experience before you move ahead.
- **Relationships** – 7 – Shih – Great Force – To lead you have to prove your worth – gain respect – work with rather than command.
- **Health** – 59 – Huan – Dispersing – Take the middle road in all things – extremes either way lead to problems – people you once knew reappear.
- **Wisdom** – 64 – Wei Chi – Before Completion – You can't finish learning until you have gathered all the facts – move forward cautiously
- **Wealth** – 47 – K'un – Adversity – Problems will occur, you cannot avoid them – stick to your guns – you will win through.

North-west-facing house

- **Fame** – 33 – Tun – Retreat – Stars shine then lose their brilliance – this is the natural order – they will shine again – withdraw and wait patiently.
- **Children** – 62 – Hsiao Kua – Great Smallness – Small is beautiful – look after the tiny details and the big events will take care of themselves.
- **Pleasure** – 39 – Chien – Obstacles – Accept obstacles as opportunities to learn – be resolved – this will pass.

☺ **Friends** – 52 – Ken – Stillness – Take time out to contemplate your situation – look at things from afar with new eyes.

☺ **Relationships** – 15 – Chien K'an – Modesty – Be moderate in your dealings with others – avoid extremes – be sincere at all costs.

☺ **Health** – 53 – Chien Li – Expanding – Take it slowly – nothing is going to happen too quickly – steady progress is the order of the day.

☺ **Wisdom** – 56 – Lu – Travel – Movement is forecast – a new period of travel and learning is likely – choose wisely.

☺ **Wealth** – 31 – Hsien – Attraction – The original wording translates as *to take a partner brings great good fortune.*

NORTH-FACING HOUSE

☺ **Fame** – 12 – P'i – Stagnation – Things are happening you know nothing about – wait and you will be rewarded – rush in and you'll fail.

☺ **Children** – 16 – Yu – Happiness – Wealth doesn't bring happiness – only inner contentment does – Follow your heart.

☺ **Pleasure** – 8 – Pi – Union – Joining together brings great joy – sharing creates links that will last – work together.

☺ **Friends** – 23 – Po – Splitting Apart – As things fall away watch them go – do nothing to hasten their falling – wait.

☺ **Relationships** – 2 – K'un – Receptive – Your future is good – others have control – trust them – it all comes well in the end.

☺ **Health** – 20 – Kuan – Watching – Observe the future – make plans – let things flow around you but don't be pulled by them.

☺ **Wisdom** – 35 – Chin – Progress – Be honest and you

can only advance – be aware of others – set a good example.

⊙ **Wealth** – 45 – Ts'ui – Gathering – Work with those around you and you can achieve great success – be cautious in what you say.

SOUTH-WEST-FACING HOUSE

⊙ **Fame** – 44 – Kou – Meeting – Be resolute – you are right – stick to your path – overcome your weaknesses to be successful.

⊙ **Children** – 32 – Heng – Endurance – Listen to others – follow old advice – others know best – stick to tried-and-tested methods.

⊙ **Pleasure** – 48 – Ching – Source – Listen to your heart – follow your instincts – you know you're right.

⊙ **Friends** – 18 – Ku – Decay – Now is the time to clear out the past – repair old hurts and move on – things will disrupt you.

⊙ **Relationships** – 46 – Sheng – Germinating – Things push upwards without you having to do anything – progress is slow – talk to others.

⊙ **Health** – 57 – Sun – Gentle – Be flexible – take things slowly – make a plan – stick to it.

⊙ **Wisdom** – 50 – Ting – Cauldron – Blend everything you know – find a new way – harmonise your wants and needs.

⊙ **Wealth** – 28 – Ta Kuo – Excess – Keep your wits about you – there's a lot going on – be confident and courageous – great success.

EAST-FACING HOUSE

⊙ **Fame** – 13 – T'ung Jen – Partnerships – What you want will be good for others – work with them – share what you know.

⊙ **Children** – 55 – Feng – Abundance – Everything is perfectly as it should be – enjoy – great good fortune and rewards.

- ☻ **Pleasure** – 63 – Chi Chi – Completion – You can rest for but a moment – then it all starts again – enjoy this quiet moment – it won't last.
- ☻ **Friends** – 22 – Pi Li – Gracefulness – Go for quality – go for style – cultivate the laconic – keep friends separate from lovers.
- ☻ **Relationships** – 36 – Ming I – Clouds – Say nothing – make plans – the sun will return – don't rise to the bait.
- ☻ **Health** – 37 – Chia Jen – Family – Trust the yin aspect – be proper – cultivate order – be ethical, moral and respectful.
- ☻ **Wisdom** – 30 – Li – Acting Together – Know your limits – utilise others – think things through – stick with what you know.
- ☻ **Wealth** – 49 – Ko – Change – Whatever your situation it will change – consider others – wealth is not just money.

SOUTH-EAST-FACING HOUSE

- ☻ **Fame** – 10 – Lu – Correctness – This is a time of great success – as long as you are correct – you know what this means.
- ☻ **Children** – 54 – Kuei Mei – Passive – Whatever you do remain quiet – you make mistakes – correct them and move along quietly – don't draw attention to yourself at this time – be passive in all things.
- ☻ **Pleasure** – 60 – Chieh – Limitations – You have to work with natural order – don't swim upstream – wait and be economical.
- ☻ **Friends** – 41 – Sun Ken – Declining – Give up a little to gain a lot – be frugal – simplify everything.
- ☻ **Relationships** – 19 – Lin – Approaching – Great growth is coming – this is a good time for you – be dynamic.
- ☻ **Health** – 61 – Chung Fu – Insights – You know the truth – now communicate it – bottling things up leads to stress – but you know that.

- **Wisdom** – 38 – K'uei – Opposing Forces – There is a dispute between what you know and what you feel – find a way to harmonise the two – be kind to yourself.
- **Wealth** – 58 – Tui – Great Joy – Others encourage you – you'll get exactly what you want – don't blow it by getting over-excited.

So, that's how the *I Ching* works with feng shui. You could do no better than to get a copy of *I Ching for Beginners* (see Further Reading) and then you can look up all these individual entries yourself.

APPENDIX I
THE FENG SHUI
COMPASS RINGS

The traditional feng shui compass has several rings of information. All the compasses vary according to the manufacturer's designs, but invariably there are three rings of essential information. The following is a list of what is on the three rings of an 'average' compass.

The Heaven Plate

1. Trigrams of Former Heaven Sequence
2. Symbols of the nine stars
3. The 24 mountains
4. The eight major planets
5. The 64 hexagrams
6. The 64 hexagrams changing
7. The 24 fortnights of the year
8. The 28 auspicious burial constellations
9. The 360 degrees of the compass
10. The 72 dragon's veins of ch'i
11. Mountains and the dragon's veins

The Human Plate

12. Stems and branches of a person's horoscope
13. The 60 points of good and bad luck
14. The spirit paths of the dead
15. Earth and mountain hexagrams for auspicious sites to live
16. Auspicious sites for burial
17. Division into the five aspects and the horoscope
18. Yin and yang
19. Auspicious river directions

APPENDIX II
FENG SHUI
ELEMENT YEARS

The Chinese new year starts on a different date each year. As a rough guide you can calculate that if you were born in a year ending in a 0 you are yang metal; 1 yin metal; 2 yang water; 3 yin water; 4 yang wood, 5 yin wood; 6 yang fire, 7 yin fire; 8 yang earth, 9 yin earth, but if you want the exact dates they are as follows.

Odd years are yin; even years are yang

Year	Element
30 Jan 1930–5 Feb 1930	Metal
6 Feb 1932–13 Feb 1934	Water
14 Feb 1934–23 Jan 1936	Wood
24 Jan 1936–30 Jan 1938	Fire
31 Jan 1938–7 Feb 1940	Earth
8 Feb 1940–14 Feb 1942	Metal
15 Feb 1942–24 Jan 1944	Water
25 Jan 1944–1 Feb 1946	Wood
2 Feb 1946–9 Feb 1948	Fire
10 Feb 1948–16 Feb 1950	Earth
17 Feb 1950–26 Jan 1952	Metal
27 Jan 1952–2 Feb 1954	Water
3 Feb 1954–11 Feb 1956	Wood
12 Feb 1956–17 Feb 1958	Fire
18 Feb 1958–27 Jan 1960	Earth
28 Jan 1960–4 Feb 1962	Metal
5 Feb 1962–12 Feb 1964	Water
13 Feb 1964 –20 Jan 1966	Wood
21 Jan 1966–29 Jan 1968	Fire

30 Jan 1968–5 Feb 1970	Earth
6 Feb 1970–15 Jan 1972	Metal
16 Jan 1972–22 Jan 1974	Water
23 Jan 1974–30 Jan 1976	Wood
31 Jan 1976 –6 Feb 1978	Fire
7 Feb 1978–15 Feb 1980	Earth
16 Feb 1980–24 Jan 1982	Metal
25 Jan 1982–1 Feb 1984	Water
2 Feb 1984–8 Feb 1986	Wood
9 Feb 1986–16 Feb 1988	Fire
17 Feb 1988–26 Jan 1990	Earth
27 Jan 1990–3 Feb 1992	Metal
4 Feb 1992–9 Feb 1994	Water
10 Feb 1994–18 Feb 1996	Wood
19 Feb 1996–27 Jan 1998	Fire
28 Jan 1998–4 Feb 2000	Earth
5 Feb 2000–11 Feb 2002	Metal

The dates listed above show the *first* and *last* days of the year inclusive.

APPENDIX III
CHINESE ANIMALS
AND THEIR ELEMENTS

Metal   dog, cockerel, monkey
Fire   goat, horse, snake
Wood   dragon, hare, tiger
Water   ox, rat, pig

The animals don't have an earth element.

Each of the animals has a 'natural' aspect to its element and whether it is yin or yang.

Pig   yin water
Rat   yang water
Ox   yin water
Tiger   yang wood
Hare   yin wood
Dragon   yang wood
Snake   yin fire
Horse   yang fire
Goat   yin fire
Monkey   yang metal
Cockerel   yin metal
Dog   yang metal

What these 'natural' aspects mean is that your best year comes round about twice in your life – if you're lucky. Suppose you were born in 1934. That would make you a Dog, and a dog is a yang metal animal. However, 1934 is a yang wood year. Your best year wouldn't have been until 1970 when you were 36 years old; 1970 is the first yang metal year that falls in the year of the Dog – which is how you calculate your 'best' year.

Suppose you were born in 1921 – a Cockerel year, and the cockerel is a yin metal animal; 1921 is also a yin metal year. In 1981 you got another best year – both cockerel and yin metal – and you will again in 2041. So if you live to be 120 years old you would have had three best years! That's very lucky indeed. The Chinese refer to this as the 60-year cycle and consider anyone born in a best year to be extremely lucky – a bit like we say someone is born with a silver spoon in their mouth – they'll want for nothing.

If you're lucky enough to be born at the right time of day you could be even more blessed. In each 24 hours there are 12 2-hour animal periods. Depending on the time you were born you have another animal to add to your own year animal. This may be called your secret animal as it reveals the 'true' you. Some say it also reveals who should be your soul mate or life companion. The times are:

11 a.m.– 1 p.m.	Horse
1 p.m.–3 p.m.	Goat
3 p.m.– 5 p.m.	Monkey
5 p.m.– 7 p.m.	Cockerel
7 p.m.– 9 p.m.	Dog
9 p.m.– 11 p.m.	Pig
11 p.m.– 1 a.m.	Rat
1 a.m.– 3 a.m.	Ox
3 a.m.– 5 a.m.	Tiger
5 a.m.– 7 a.m.	Dragon
9 a.m.– 11 a.m.	Snake

And don't forget that each of these animals has its own compass direction which may give you a clue as to which season, direction, time of day and month you feel 'right' in. This is all classical, astrological feng shui.

Chart of directions and further information

This chart gives compatibility, times of the day we may feel best at, best house directions, areas of human development that concern us most, and a comparison of Eastern with Western astrology.

Ken							
Tzu	Marriage	Rat	Water	11p.m.–1 a.m.	North	January	Aquarius
Ch'ou	Emotion	Ox	Metal	1–3 a.m.	NNE	February	Pisces
Yin	Energy	Tiger	Fire	3–5 a.m.	NE	March	Aries
H'sun							
Mao	Wisdom	Hare	Wood	5–7 a.m.	East	April	Taurus
Chen	Sex	Dragon	Water	7–9 a.m.	SSE	May	Gemini
Ssu	Wealth	Snake	Metal	9–11 a.m.	SE	June	Cancer
K'un							
Wu	Fame	Horse	Fire	11 a.m.–1 p.m.	South	July	Leo
Wei	Peace	Sheep	Wood	1–3 p.m.	SSW	August	Virgo
Shen	Health	Monkey	Water	3–5 p.m.	SW	September	Libra
Ch'ien							
Yu	Life	Cock	Metal	5–7 p.m.	West	October	Scorpio
Hsu	Travel	Dog	Fire	7–9 p.m.	NNW	November	Sagittarius
Hai	Friends	Pig	Wood	9–11 p.m.	NW	December	Capricorn

GLOSSARY

An Lu south-west direction, peace and happiness
Arrowed killing ch'i three straight lines of ch'i
   converging to a point
ch'i energy
Ch'ien The Creative, heaven, south, summer
chai dwelling, houses
Chang Yin west, pleasure and indulgence, dangerous
Chen The Arousing, wood, north-east, thunder
chin metal
Chin Ts'ai north-west, new beginnings
Chin Yin north, relationships
enrichments the eight areas of life situations
Fa Chan east, wisdom and experience
fan ch'i offensive ch'i, residual emotions
fang inner
feng wind
Feng Huang the Red Phoenix of the south
feng shui wind/water, Chinese geomancy
feng shui hsien-sheng a feng shui consultant or
   practitioner
H'sun – The Wind, gentle, south-west, wood
hsin heart, ourselves
hsueh surroundings
Huan Lo south-east, wealth
huo fire
I Ching the Book of Changes
Jen Hsin the Centre
K'an The Dangerous, water, west, autumn, the moon
K'un The Receptive, creation, north, winter
Ken The Stillness, mountain, north-west, calm
killing ch'i ch'i flowing too fast in a straight line

Li The Clinging, fire, east, spring, the sun

liu trees, gardens, willows

lo shu the magic square

lo p'an the feng shui compass

lung mei the dragon's veins, paths of ch'i

mu wood

Pah Kwa the great symbol (yin/yang symbol with the eight trigrams)

sha unhealthy ch'i

sha ch'i disruptive ch'i from the west

shan mountains

shan shui mountains and water, style of Chinese landscape painting

shao yang east or lesser yang

shao yin west or lesser yin

sheng ch'i growing ch'i from the east

shui water

t'ai ch'i the Supreme Ultimate

t'ai ch'i chuan Chinese martial art

t'ai yang south or great yang

t'ai yin north or great yin

T'ien Ch'ai north-east, children and family

t'sang ch'i hidden ch'i from the north

t'u earth

Tao the Way, a religion, philosophy, way of life, the Universal Principle

ts'ang feng cold, hidden wind that blows from hollows and can cause ill health

Tui The Lake, metal, south-east, joy

Wang Ts'ai south, prosperity and fame

Wen the Green Dragon of the East

Wu the White Tiger of the West

wu hsing the five aspects or elements

yang creative energy

yang ch'i nourishing ch'i from the south

yin receptive energy

Yuan Wu the Black Tortoise of the north

FURTHER READING

Feng shui

An Anthropological Analysis of Chinese Geomancy, Stephen Feuchtwang, SMC, 1974.

Change your Life with Feng Shui, Li Pak Tin and Helen Yeap, Quantum, 1997.

Feng Shui, Angel Thompson, St Martin's Griffin, 1995.

Feng Shui, Kirsten M. Lagatree, Newleaf, 1996.

Feng Shui for Beginners, Richard Craze, Hodder & Stoughton, 1996.

Feng Shui Made Easy, William Spear, Thorsons, 1995.

Interior Design with Feng Shui, Sarah Rossbach, Rider Books, 1987.

Practical Feng Shui, Richard Craze, Anness, 1997.

The Complete Illustrated Guide to Feng Shui, Lillian Too, Element Books, 1996.

The Elements of Feng Shui, Man-Ho Kwok with Joanne O'Brien, Element Books, 1991.

The Feng Shui Game Pack, Richard Craze, Godsfield Press and HarperCollins, 1997.

The Feng Shui Kit, Man-Ho Kwok, Piatkus, 1995.

The Feng Shui Pack, Richard Craze, Godsfield Press and HarperCollins, 1997.

The Living Earth Manual of Feng Shui, Chinese Geomancy, Stephen Skinner, Arkana, 1982.

The Western Guide to Feng Shui, Terah Kathryn Collins, Hay House Inc., 1995.

Chinese Philosophy

Between Heaven and Earth, Harriet Beinfield and Efrem Korngold, Ballantine Books, 1991.

Chinese Astrology, Collins Gem, 1996.

Chinese Horoscopes for Beginners, Kristyna Arcarti, Hodder & Stoughton, 1995.

Chinese Mythology, Derek Walters, The Aquarian Press, 1992.

I Ching for Beginners, Kristyna Arcarti, Hodder & Stoughton, 1994.

Lao Tzu's TAO TE CHING, edited Timothy Freke, Piatkus, 1995.

Teach Yourself Chinese Astrology, Richard Craze, Hodder & Stoughton, 1997.

The Fundamental Principles of the Yi-king Tao, Veolita Parke Boyle, W & G Foyle, 1934.

The I Ching and Mankind, Diana ffarington Hook, Routledge and Kegan Paul, 1975.

The I Ching Workbook, R. L. Wing, Aquarian, 1983.

The Secret of the Golden Flower, Richard Wilhelm, Routledge and Kegan Paul, 1974.

The Way of Life, Witter Bynner, Perigee Books, 1944.

Chinese Health

Chi Kung, James MacRitchie, Element, 1995.

Chinese Herbal Medicine, Richard Craze, Piatkus, 1996.

Teach Yourself Traditional Chinese Medicine, Richard Craze, Hodder & Stoughton, 1997.

The Complete Illustrated Guide to Chinese Medicine, Tom Williams, Element Books, 1997.

General

Cambridge Illustrated History of China, Patricia Buckley Ebrey, Cambridge University Press, 1996.

China, Land of Discovery and Invention, Robert Temple, Patrick Stephens, 1986.

Imperial China, Charis Chan, Penguin Books, 1991.

The Changing Society of China, Ch'u Chai and Winberg Chai, Mentor Books, 1962.

USEFUL ADDRESSES

United Kingdom
Feng Shui Network International
PO Box 2133
London W1A 1RL

Feng Shui Society
18 Alacross Road
London W5 4HT

Feng Shui Association
31 Woburn Place
Brighton
East Sussex BN1 9GA

The Feng Shui Company
Ballard House
37 Norway Street
Greenwich
London SE10 9DD

Australia
Feng Shui Design Studio
PO Box 705
Glebe
Sydney NSW 2037

Feng Shui Society of Australia
PO Box 1565
Rozelle
Sydney NSW 2039

North America
Earth Design
PO Box 530725
Miami Shore
Florida 33153

The Feng Shui Institute of America
PO Box 488
Wabasso
Florida 32970

Feng Shui Warehouse
PO Box 3005
San Diego
California 92163

Surf the Net with feng shui

At the time of writing there are some 5,968 relevant documents about feng shui on the Internet. These are but a few of them, selected to give you some addresses to get you started.

http://www.lmcinet.com/amfengshui
American Feng Shui Institute's Home Page web site.

http://www.ozemail.com.au./bmtv/fengshui.htm
Feng shui advice, videos, newsletters, remedies.

htp://downtown.wcb.aol.com/ads/cats/cat_home garden7txt.html
Home and garden feng shui, including bonsai trees.

http://www.spiritweb.org/Spirit/feng-shui-liu-07.html
Feng shui and love. Promotes spiritual consciousness on the Internet. Healing schools and techniques of feng shui and ch'i.

http://www.spiritweb.org/Spirit/feng-shui-liu-05.html
Feng Shui and astrology.

http://www.fsgallery.com/
Feng shui gallery of calligraphy and art. A gallery of Chinese and Japanese art and calligraphy.

http://www.cwo.com/~ashlin/shui8.html
Feng Shui: The Chinese art of design and placement reviews. Two internationally sought-after consultants offer a history of this venerable art, guidance on how to use it effectively.

http://www.mistral.co.uk./hammerwood/dowser.htm
Feng shui, earth acupuncture, geomancy, dowsing, geopathic stress, white and black streams, healing streams, ley lines, earth mysteries, earth healing, watercourses, underground water.

http://www.meltzerfengshui.com/
Creating heaven on earth. Carol Meltzer Feng Shui Designs. Functional Art Gallery.

http://www.cwo.com/~ashlin/flutes.html"
Feng shui flutes and word stones.

http://www.asiaconnect.com.my/lillian-too/fundamental/
Fundamentals of feng shui – the Trinity of Luck, Order and Form.

http://www.community.net/~sgxenja/index.html
Seann Xenja's home page. Welcome to the world of feng shui. The Web site of a feng shui consultant.

http://www.intersurf.com/locale/geo/
Geomancy Dragon Feng Shui Education Organisation.